This b...

Please return ...
read
078910 76763

© Pat Thielen

About the Author

Jaya Jaya Myra is an internationally published writer, speaker, healer and activist of sacred lifestyle. Her teachings help people to realize the Self and God within through individual dharma and lifepath, by living empowered, integrated lives. She emphasizes a conscious Shakti perspective of integrated dynamic living that embraces every part of life (including career, relationships, sex, money, power and matter) as a powerful component of one's spiritual pursuit.

Myra's teachings cater to the problems individuals and societies currently face with an emphasis on teaching the character development necessary to live a fully empowered, conscious lifestyle. She works with people to overcome obstacles, maintain radiant physical health, develop a confident Self-image, and have the courage to make a difference in this world.

Visit her online at www.hridaya-healing.com and www.gitaforthemasses.org.

vibrational
Healing

·························

Attain Balance & Wholeness

◆

Understand Your Energetic Type

JAYA JAYA MYRA

Llewellyn Publications
Woodbury, Minnesota

FIRST EDITION
First Printing, 2015

Book design by Bob Gaul
Cover design by Ellen Lawson
Cover images: Thinkstock/179221074/©tr3gi, Thinkstock/142095986/©Ivary,
        iStockphoto.com/139915/©Dominic Current
Chakra illustration: Mary Ann Zapalac
Editing by Ed Day
Flower graphic © *"Old Fashioned Floral Designs: CD-ROM and Book,"*
        Dover Publications, 1990, Toronto, Ontario

Llewellyn Publications is a registered trademark of Llewellyn Worldwide Ltd.

Library of Congress Cataloging-in-Publication Data
Myra, Jaya Jaya, 1979–
  Vibrational healing, attain balance & wholeness: understand your energetic
type/Jaya Jaya Myra.—First edition.
    pages cm
  ISBN 978-0-7387-4362-2
1. Energy medicine. 2. Vibration—Therapeutic use. 3. Healing. I. Title.
  RZ421.M97 2015
  615.8'52—dc23
                    2014040976

Llewellyn Publications does not participate in, endorse, or have any authority
or responsibility concerning private business transactions between our authors
and the public.

All mail addressed to the author is forwarded, but the publisher cannot, unless
specifically instructed by the author, give out an address or phone number.

Any Internet references contained in this work are current at publication time,
but the publisher cannot guarantee that a specific location will continue to be
maintained. Please refer to the publisher's website for links to authors' websites
and other sources. Cover model(s) used for illustrative purposes only and may
not endorse or represent the book's subject.

Llewellyn Publications
A Division of Llewellyn Worldwide Ltd.
2143 Wooddale Drive
Woodbury, MN 55125-2989
www.llewellyn.com

Printed in the United States of America

Contents

Introduction

My name is Myra. I'm a writer, healer, and spiritual guide. I've written this book on vibrational healing to give a well-rounded perspective on what healing is, how it works on all levels of being (mind, body, and soul), and how to begin facilitating a healing process in your life that works for you. Vibrational healing is a system that utilizes the subtle energy found within ourselves and nature as a tool toward healing. Plants, stones, water, sound, and most everything you can find, including yourself, has energy inside of it, which can be used to restore health and well-being on a mental, emotional, and physical level.

Fundamentally, when mind, body, and soul are unified, the subtle energy we have inside of us flows freely. Whenever one of these pieces becomes out of balance with the others, there is no longer a natural flow to life or to the subtle energy within the body. When all parts of being are not unified, energetic stagnation and blockages are formed. Vibrational healing helps move inner stagnant energy so it can flow freely, which helps an individual to become balanced and healthy on all levels of being. It also recognizes that different approaches work for different physical body types and different temperaments, making it a robust system of healing.

Everything is interconnected through overlapping vibrational frequency. In vibrational healing, different forms of subtle energy are used to restore health and well-being on a mental, emotional, and physical level. Since the body is made up of subtle energy, all forms of energy can have an impact on the body, whether they come from an external or internal source. Take a moment to contemplate this. Whatever is happening within a person's subtle energy, thoughts, and emotions will also be reflected through the physical body. Pains, ailments, and diseases are areas in consciousness where things have gone awry from their source of being and are out of balance. By the time this starts expressing itself on a physical level, the imbalance has become severe. Energy works its way outward from very subtle to increasing levels of being tangible. In other words, it means the imbalance has permeated every other level of being before it affects the physical body.

There is a great piece of wisdom that says the inner being affects the outer reality. The opposite is also equally as true—outer reality can affect the inner being. Plants, herbs, stones, and more have an impact on overall health.

When things get out of balance inwardly, using an external source of vibrational energy to restore balance is the quickest and most effective way to facilitate healing. The world is here to provide support, and there are many, many external modalities available to restore health and happiness to life.

How I Came to Vibrational Healing

I have been deeply interested in both spirituality and healing since I was a small child. As I was growing up, I had dreams of becoming a doctor and healing many people or becoming a minister. Later in life, I became interested in research and science. I dreamed of finding a cure for cancer or AIDS. I've always had a difficult time seeing people suffer and have always wanted to alleviate the pain of others. I had a difficult life growing up and endured a combination of emotional and sexual abuse. Luckily for me, it was a catalyst that made me stronger and more determined to never give up.

When I was halfway through college, I gave birth to my oldest daughter. At that point, I decided medical school would be too rigorous to allow me to properly care for a family. I decided to continue with my scientific degree and entered a PhD program in Cell and Molecular Biology. Close to the point where all of my coursework, except for my thesis, was complete, I met my first real guru and spiritual teacher. While I can't put that experience into words, I instantly knew that what I really wanted in my heart would not come from being a scientist or a doctor. Gradually, then rapidly, my life shifted. I worked in the pharmaceutical industry in an area that dealt with animal testing in both rodents and primates. I was good at what I did, but bringing death to creatures in the name of health and wellness took a huge toll on me emotionally. One day, I couldn't take it anymore. I had no idea what to do, but I knew I couldn't harm another animal. I prayed that my hands would stop working, just so I didn't have to go dose another animal.

Well, it happened. I got there and my hands literally went numb and stopped working. At that point, some very mysterious occurrences began happening in my life on both a spiritual and physical level, and I continued to grow more and more physically ill. I was released from my job on disability. None of the tests or doctors could determine one thing wrong with me! I was in horrible pain, but had no definitive diagnosis. This was the point in my life that I lost everything. My job, my home, my marriage ... everything; I prayed fiercely for a change, and a change is exactly what I got, although it was not the change I had expected or wanted. Even though my life had suddenly collapsed and things were much more challenging, and chaotic, I found myself much happier and feeling more on the right life path.

But I still had the pain, and pharmaceutical drugs made me worse. Eventually, I knew I either had to find another way or end up dead. I went through about a five-year journey toward health and healing. I became a certified yoga instructor and yoga therapist. I learned Reiki and other forms of subtle energy healing. I changed my diet. I meditated every day. I adhered to a strict daily practice focused on healing my mind, body, and soul. It took a lot of time, a lot of tears, and a lot of discipline, but it worked. I became clearer, stronger, more filled with love and joy and less with fear. As I changed and grew through my experiences, I became able to help others in the ways I really wanted to be able to help. People started coming to me for guidance and healing, and I started my path as a healer and spiritual guide.

I've had the opportunity to do a lot of great things and my life has completely changed for the better. While I didn't become a doctor or scientist, I have gotten exactly what I wanted as a child; through my spiritual practice and life's experiences, I've learned the core essence of healing and how to connect directly with the God in my own heart. I've worked with many women who have undergone physical and sexual abuse, people who are discouraged and confused in life, and people who just deep down need to know how loved they really are. I moved from the West Coast to New York City to start a spiritual and healing center. I've founded a nonprofit called Gita for the Masses, which teaches people how to overcome obstacles and become victorious in life. I get to appear on TV regularly discussing spirituality and healing. I've spoken at the United Nations on spirituality and women's empowerment. I write constantly about the spiritual side of life and how to integrate spirituality into everyday life, both for magazines and for my nonprofit organization. Being a healer and guide is my life's calling, and I am extremely grateful to have the opportunities and experiences I have been given. Both the good and bad situations in my life have taught me how to effectively work with others.

Try Something New

Vibrational healing may be a very new concept for you. In exploring the process of health and healing, self-knowledge is crucial. In order to get to know yourself, you have to take chances and try new things. It's from this place of knowing oneself and acting in alignment with one's own innate character that all health and well-being comes from. Only when you know yourself can you be effective in working with subtle energy. The exercises outlined in chapter 3 about determining your elemental and temperament composition are an excellent starting point, but ultimately each and every person will have to go out on a limb and try something new. Even if it's not clear which approach is best, go out and try something! You might surprise yourself and end up completely loving something you never thought you'd have an interest in.

For a person who is really serious about experiencing the benefits of energy healing, I recommend trying several different modalities—even ones that are on the bottom of your list. Instead of letting the mind think it knows something, validate or negate its thoughts through direct experience. Give every modality you try a fair chance—don't just try something once or twice. To really gauge its effectiveness, let it work on the human system for some time before jumping to something else. It takes the mind approximately six weeks to start breaking old habits and several months to get established into a new groove of thinking and living.

How to Use This Book

This book is my first attempt to take some rather esoteric spiritual laws and explain them in a practical and beneficial way for overall health and well-being in life. I hope it will help you understand some aspects of healing that are essential to know, but are rarely discussed in such a clear, candid fashion. Nothing in this book is meant to take the place of introspection and deep contemplation. Everything presented here is an excellent starting point to make you think and delve in deeper to your own study of life and health.

In this book, we will take a look at all sorts of healing modalities and work to understand which ones are right for you and why they are right for you based on elemental composition and on a person's temperament or character. We will dive into the basic concepts of health and energy, how to understand your whole self, and how to work with the innate healing energy every person has within them. We will also explore how inner temperament connects to external healing tools and modalities so that you can understand what works for you and why.

In part 1 we will discuss how to determine your unique energy type. Chapter 1 will discuss the basis of vibrational healing as an integrated and balanced person. We will look at how the mind, heart, and feelings all relate and work together to build a healthy lifestyle. Chapter 1 will also discuss the importance of inner prosperity in health and healing and the differences between the Eastern and Western approaches to wellness. In chapter 2, we will learn what subtle energy is and where it comes from, and also take a look at ten chakras in the body and their role in maintaining good health. Chapter 3 will discuss how to understand your energy type and temperament by learning about the gunas and elements. Chapter 3 is also where you will find two quizzes to help you determine your specific temperament and body type.

In part 2, we will delve into learning tools and techniques for healing. Chapter 4 will discuss healing modalities according to physical body type and the elements. Chapter 5 will discuss healing modalities as they relate to temperament, life purpose, and the gunas. Chapter 6 gives specific practices to begin with that correlate to different elements and gunas as a way to start you on your healing journey. There is also an appendix specifically geared toward healers, discussing some important concepts of what makes a person a good healer.

Before you dive into the details to come, I want to share a secret with you first; ensure it forms the basis of your entire journey in vibrational healing. It's the return to balance that facilitates well-being, which means it is our own intention—our own integrity and willpower—that heals us. Every external or internal thing we use is just a tool to facilitate that process, whether it is an herb, music, or any other healing implement. There is no energy that exists outside of you that does not also exist inside of you. It's ultimately up to you alone to be healed and to have the determination, the character, the life balance, and the willpower necessary to reach that point. People and tools can assist greatly in this process, but the final decision to be well lies within you. Now, let's have some fun exploring how to get there.

part one

The Basics of Health & Energy

Life is diverse. No two people choose to live in the same way, yet we all have similar overarching desires and big-picture questions. At some point in life, everyone will ask themselves these questions, many of which revolve around health and well-being. How to be truly healthy and balanced in life is perhaps the most important question to ask, since it impacts all other aspects of life.

Health and well-being is still an elusive topic in the collective societal consciousness. There are so many approaches to being healthy, and many of these approaches contradict one another. Despite this, you'll find determined people on both ends of the spectrum and everywhere in between asserting their way is the right way and the best way. To make matters even more confusing, you can find people at each end of the spectrum, and everywhere in between, that have had success in their approach. Different things have proven themselves to work for different people, and what works for one person has also been shown not to work for another. There is more to the process of healing than meets the eye.

I don't believe there is a right way or best way to approach healing and throughout this book we will explore the many reasons why. To put it succinctly, we are all so diverse and unique that it is impossible to delineate one specific approach to health and well-being that will work for everyone, 100 percent of the time. Even as unique individuals, we constantly grow and change with time. Inclinations change, desires change, likes and dislikes come and go. We all go through distinct phases of psychological and emotional growth as well as biological changes in life where our perceptions and realities change, sometimes drastically. All of these things affect our overall health and are as unique to each and every individual as a person's hopes and dreams.

However, while our psychology, emotions, and desires change over time, our overall body type and core temperament do not, which makes focusing on these two things an excellent approach to health and healing. By understanding yourself, you can learn to heal yourself during all of the life stages and transitions that occur. In this section, we will discuss how to determine your unique energy type, look at ten important chakras to healing, learn about gunas and elements, and how these determine your body type and temperament. We will also learn specifically what subtle energy is, where it comes from, and how mind, heart, and feelings all contribute to making a person healthy and balanced in life.

It's time to create a life of health, prosperity, and soul-filled living. Are you ready?

one

The Basis of
Vibrational Healing

· · · · · · · · · · · · · ·

The journey to healing and wholeness is one of the most exciting journeys a person can embark upon. It's a life-long process of learning, experiencing, and delving into who and what you are and learning how life and experience impacts you. Healing is such a broad topic, so there are many things to consider in your journey. In this chapter, we will take a conceptual look at what vibrational healing is and how it differs from conventional modes of therapy. We will discuss the mind, intellect, heart, feelings, and spiritual components of well-being. All of these components play a role in health. The root essence of vibrational healing is to restore balance to all levels of a person's being. Having conceptual clarity of how all of these pieces work individually and how they work together will enable healing to be more complete and more effective. Let's begin!

Vibrational Healing & the Integrated Person

People are complex. We have a whole mind, body, soul complex to consider when contemplating the whole spectrum of wellness, and vibrational healing is no exception. Vibrational healing is a methodology of healing that uses subtle energy to restore balance on a mind, body, or emotional level. Vibrational healing has so many different approaches, but the fundamental essence is the same—our bodies are made up of different subtle energy currents (or vibrations) that work together as a unified whole. When the unified whole person becomes out of balance, disease or "dis-ease" occurs because of stagnant energy. Any disharmony between thoughts, feelings, body, mind, and soul is the root cause of stagnant energy in the body, which can lead to disease.

All things here on Earth have a certain vibration and energy field. When you learn to use something—be that an herb, a stone, music, touch, or any other thing (including yourself and your own energy)—as a modality of wellbeing, you are working with the concepts of vibrational healing. Vibrational healing works to restore balance to the mind, body, and emotions by helping make stagnant energy flow freely. In order to be integrated and whole and find deep fulfillment in life, all of our being has to be in resonance and harmony with itself, working as a unified whole being. These concepts of integration and wholeness are what spiritual seekers refer to as unity. Everything that you are, think, feel, believe, and experience has to work in tandem with each other, not against one another.

Our bodies and everything here on Earth are made up of a combination of the elements of nature: earth, water, fire, air, and ether. All elemental and material frequencies start in an individual's core consciousness and are then differentiated into diverse frequencies out of this one source consciousness, which some people refer to as the soul, and even God. The elements are not the only frequency of vibration, but because they determine the physical structure of the body, they have a huge impact on well-being. When done effectively, all forms of vibrational healing take the whole being, the entire mind, body, soul complex into account. Both elemental vibrations and those that relate to a person's temperament or character can be used to facilitate healing and overall well-being.

The fact that we all grow and evolve through time makes being an integrated, whole person a process in and of itself. Just when you've figured out what it means to be yourself and fulfill your desires and needs, things change! Life is dynamic! Being integrated and whole changes as our needs and desires change. Whether or not a person has the capacity to live an integrated life depends almost exclusively on how well a person develops their character and innate temperament. By character, I am referring to some basic traits of successful living such as fearlessness, courage, self-honesty, clarity, discipline, and confidence. These traits are part of every human being's innate potential, but this potential must be cultivated for integration to become possible. When a person develops the capacity to truly know what they want and need in life and are willing to put in the effort to get it (this is where discipline and consistency come in), nothing is impossible.

The more a person divides their energy in different directions, the more difficult it is to accomplish anything. The same thing happens within the body and the psyche— when inner conflict increases, the ability to be whole and complete decreases. Conflict prevents happiness; it creates doubt and it leads to emotional turbulence. This lack of inner balance, or what I would call character, has a major impact on a whole person, including the body.

In our bodies, we have diverse organ systems that all work together in harmony, even though each organ system is unique and serves an important function: the overall mind, body, soul complex functions in the same way. When mind, body, and soul don't work together, disharmony manifests. If your heart decided to tell your liver it isn't good enough and to take a hike, what would happen? We do this constantly in regards to our integrated being. We as people convince ourselves, or are convinced by others, that pieces of ourselves aren't important, which leads to suffering and disharmony. Since all of it is a part of the intrinsic nature of your whole being, when one piece suffers, the rest suffer too.

The concept of living an integrated, whole life is very simple. Simple, however, does not mean it's easy. It's probably the simplicity of this concept that makes people take it too lightly. Integration is the capacity to do a lot of different little things and put them together to work as a whole. To the mind, this is an overwhelming concept. That's because mind can be described as only the surface of the heart—because it is only a piece of the whole, the mind cannot comprehend the whole. Yet we have grown up giving the mind much more control than it should be allowed to command. (I will talk about the mind and heart in much greater depth in a bit.) The capacity to live an integrated life comes from a much deeper place that will force a more holistic balance between the entire mind, body, soul complex.

For balance and integration, the needs of the whole must be considered. This means a balance between the physical body and what its unique structure needs, the mind (which includes sensory perceptions), and feelings and the spirit (or soul) that connects everything. Since people in our modern culture have a tendency to be controlled by the mind, it can take a lot of hard work and effort to return to a state of harmony between these three major components of our being.

When we function as integrated, whole people, health and wellness is a natural result. When there is imbalance and inner conflict, it can eventually lead to problems in the physical body that show up as disease. This is where the Eastern and Western approaches to physical health take different directions, and because they are divergent, it is important to have clarity of both paradigms to make informed decisions.

Western vs. Eastern Approach to Healing

How often in your life have you experienced something that could not be identified or treated by a doctor? Did having this sort of experience ever make you wonder about what disease or pain really is and where it comes from, or if answers to these questions even exist? These sorts of questions are probably what have you pursuing some knowledge of vibrational healing and learning how it differs from conventional medicine. The Western approach toward healing is very different from the Eastern approach. A Western medical doctor will work to "cure" someone of a disease or illness, where someone utilizing Eastern approaches will work to bring balance to "dis-ease" through bringing the mind, body, and soul back into balance. The Western approach is based on scientific and intellectual understanding alone whereas the Eastern approach looks at the entire mind, body, soul complex. Through the Eastern approach, it is understood that the soul is the foundation for the rest of subtle energy and even the physical body. Since Western medicine cannot prove the existence of the soul or subtle energy, neither are taken into consideration and the entire approach is different.

The Western medical system sees a disease solely in terms of its physical manifestations. And because the focal point is the physical illness itself, the target is in eliminating the physical manifestation by any means possible. Oftentimes this involves the use of treatments that are extremely toxic that throw the rest of the body out of balance. Radiation and chemotherapy used in cancer treatments are excellent examples of this. They cause extreme sickness, fatigue, and many other problems because there is no way to contain such a harsh poison to just the diseased area itself.

The Eastern approach to health and well-being is much different; the Eastern approach sees an illness or disease as merely a symptom the mind, body, soul complex is no longer in harmony, but these symptoms are not viewed as the root cause or even the disease itself. The imbalance of the mind, body, and soul are believed to be the dis-ease, which is caused by subtle energy in the body becoming trapped or stagnant. This stagnant energy is believed to cause the physical manifestations of illness because they are areas that are not being nourished by healthy, flowing energy. In an Eastern approach, the focal point is rarely on destroying the particular disease manifestation; it's on establishing a strong and healthy flow of energy.

Everything is taken into consideration in an Eastern approach. How is your marriage or family life? Are you happy in life? Are you fulfilled in your career or life pursuits? Do you have a spiritual practice as a part of your daily routine? Are you getting adequate exercise for your physical body? Have you experienced something traumatic that needs to be worked through? All of this is seen as important to the overall picture of someone's health.

The Eastern approach works to strengthen the particular area of the mind, body, soul complex that is out of balance; it believes that once balance is restored and stuck energy (known as prana or chi) is made to move freely, health will automatically be restored by the body itself. The body and its subtle energy system are seen as tremendous life-giving forces of their own that when treated well can take care of the body with no problems. Correcting a problem in the body may mean primarily targeting the mind or emotions as the key to establishing balance. It may mean a change of diet, eliminating a constricting belief pattern, or adopting a hobby that contributes to happiness. It may mean getting out of an abusive life situation or cultivating a means of artistic, creative expression. The whole approach focuses on the body as a great innate life-giving mechanism that can heal itself when a person lives a balanced and fulfilling life.

While it all fundamentally comes down to balance, it is important to understand that vibrational healing approaches recognize that different therapies are used for different psychological and physical temperaments, which will be discussed in depth in later chapters. You can think of each and every person as having a unique psychological inclination, which is also reflected through unique emotions and unique body types or physical constitution. It's a person's unique temperament and constitution that determines what life balance is appropriate.

I have absolutely no doubt that in time, science will be able to understand and even prove how vibrational healing works. They are starting to even now; well, maybe not understand it, but evidence of how even meditation has positive effects on health cannot be denied. The Eastern approach to well-being has never left out the spiritual or soul component that creates the overall consciousness of an individual and one day, the Western paradigm won't be able to either. It will have to evolve into something more refined or become obsolete. Let me give you a practical example. Did you know that a well-trained Ayurvedic practitioner or a person versed in the art of kinesiology can do a pulse diagnosis and determine exactly what is out of balance in the body and what is causing it? No other diagnostic tool is necessary. No blood work or expansive scans. This is highly entertaining in light of the fact that Western doctors know we have a pulse...and that's it. Even this one small bit of information in itself, if it were more widely known and accepted in society, would shake the foundation of Western medicine as we know it.

The Mind & Overall Health

The mind is one of the most powerful tools in existence, yet it is also one of the most misunderstood. Whether or not vibrational healing will work, and the extent to which it works, completely depends on the mind. The mind is separated into two distinct components in the subtle body: Manas and Indu. Manas deals with sensory impressions, habits, and conditioning, whereas Indu deals with the intellect, the capacity for expansion, inner discernment, and dissolution of inner negativity. For clarity and conceptual understanding, when I use the word "mind," I am referring to Manas and when I speak of the intellect, inner discernment, or self-inquiry, I am referring to Indu.

The moment you question yourself, "Is this really me, or is this just my mind?" you will certainly understand the differentiations between you, your mind, and your intellect. When you experience firsthand how powerfully a habit has control over you, you'll also understand this. I love to wake up in the morning and move. If I don't, my whole day feels out of balance. This feeling of being out of balance comes from the mind not getting what it is accustomed to. This habit is neither good nor bad, but how it affects me and my feelings the rest of the day is an excellent example of the habituated mind.

The Manas mind governs the conscious part of life, the instinctual self and subconscious mind that stores emotions and sensory impressions. It is the patterned, habitual aspect of the mind. Let's look at how this benefits and hinders us. When people think and act in life, both conscious and subconscious patterns affect how we choose to act, live, and respond to all of life's situations. We, however, are only aware of what is going on in the conscious part of the mind. The subconscious, or habitual, mind acts without us even being aware of it; this is what makes it "sub-conscious," or below the perception of the "conscious" mind.

Even though the conscious mind seems to make the decisions on a daily basis, the subconscious mind greatly influences how we react to situations, but in more subtle ways. We get accustomed to patterns and habits, and certain ways of perceiving life become innate to our being. When you go onto autopilot and respond in a certain way without thinking about it, this is the subconscious mind at work. When something becomes second nature and requires little to no effort, it has become subconscious. The subconscious always affects how you act and perceive the world and because its actions are no longer a conscious response to life, it is important to understand its habituated patterns.

The patterned, habitual aspect of the mind forms the foundation of how we live life. All of our sensory experiences and the feelings they generate get locked into the mind and create thought forms. It is these thought forms that form the basis for all reaction patterns and habitual responses in life. After some time, the impressions go dormant and the conscious mind forgets them, but the subconscious does not. Thought forms create grooves in the mind—the more impactful the feeling, the deeper the groove. Energy travels along these grooves, so if the experience that created the groove was not a positive one, it's important to get rid of it. Just as a groove is created, it can be filled in through healing, meditation, and a variety of other techniques designed to restore balance and well-being to the mind.

The mind is an excellent thing for someone who is disciplined and on a very positive, proactive life path. Just as we can program our minds to be happy and positive, we can also program them to be unhappy and unhealthy. This is where the mind becomes a double-edged sword. The mind is a powerful tool that will do what it is conditioned to do. When people continually feel unhappy, this eventually works its way into the subconscious mind and these feelings of unhappiness become the norm. It then takes consistent conscious effort to be happy. I'm sure you've heard the saying, whatever you focus on you will eventually become. The Manas mind is why!

The intellect is what governs the capacity for both creativity and dissolution. When the intellect (Indu) is directed outward, it creates brilliant things and ideas. When the intellect is directed inward, it governs the process of dissolution of thought forms stored in the Manas portion of the mind. How this works could fill an entire book in and of itself, so I'll just discuss the basic aspects here. When the intellect focuses inward toward the core self and soul, it is capable of distinguishing the soul from the thought forms that have been created in the Manas mind by the senses. The intellect is what brings perspective to the stored impressions of the mind, allowing the overall being some separation from the habits and tendencies we form.

Using the intellect in an inward, pointed fashion of self-inquiry to dissolve thought forms happens in a series of steps, the first of which is to be aware of the presence of a thought form. This is easiest to first recognize by becoming aware that you have a habitual reaction to a specific situation. As an example, let's look at Sally and her fear of dogs. Every time she sees one, her heart starts racing, her breathing grows shallow, and she gets fearful. She remembers having no fear of dogs until she was chased and bitten by one when she was five years old, but after that incident, every time she sees a dog, she becomes afraid. This is even true if she knows the specific dog in question is well mannered and friendly.

Thought forms create reaction patterns that lead us to not being capable of being present in the moment at hand. Even though Sally knows fully well her best friend's dog named Rufus is well trained and will not bite her, she is still afraid. The fear is not technically toward Rufus, but is elicited from the stored impression and memory she carries from being bitten as a child. Rufus just acts as a catalyst to reawaken this stored impression. This is the process of becoming aware.

Step two is in learning to recondition the mind through forming a new reaction pattern. By learning to use the intellect powerfully, you can retrain the patterned mind to eliminate negative stored impressions that form grooves in the mind. Here's how Sally works toward that. Since Sally knows her fear is based in the past and is not due to her present circumstance, and she knows Rufus is friendly, Sally makes the concerted effort to befriend Rufus and play with him every time she visits her friend. Over time, Sally is able to overcome her fear of dogs because she has retrained her mind not to be afraid. The new sensory impressions and positive feelings gained from interacting with Rufus act to dissolve the thought form that caused her to be afraid of dogs.

Let's be clear; this process takes both time and consistency. It also involves the realm of feeling, which will be discussed in the next section on the heart. Since the event that created the thought form in this example was traumatic in nature, it has more initial energy than the situation where Sally was timidly trying to befriend Rufus. Newton's first and second laws can be used to understand this concept; an object in motion will stay in motion until an opposing force acts to stop its momentum. If force equals mass times velocity, it takes an equal and opposing force to elicit an opposite response. In other words, it took Sally a lot of concerted effort at peace building with Rufus to equal the force of the initial traumatic situation that caused the fear. The concerted effort over time added up and acted to halt the momentum of the initial reaction.

Sally's example shows how to get the intellect working in a positive, inward way for bringing balance back to the mind. For many of the conditioned responses you will learn to recognize, you won't necessarily know what caused them, but you will be able to tell your reaction is a conditioned reaction and not a conscious response in the moment at hand. That is the difference between reaction and response. Reaction is conditioned whereas response looks at everything equally in the present moment—with no bias from the past. Beyond the initial stages of learning how to use the intellect, it really does not matter if you know what caused the initial thought form or not. Once you recognize you have a reaction pattern, you can work to change it into something positive or eliminate it altogether.

By learning to use the Indu portion of the mind, which governs intellect and self-inquiry, the Manas mind can be brought back to a neutral, unconditioned state of being. We don't have to be dragged through life feeling out of control of our thoughts and feelings. Just as food needs to be digested, thoughts and thought forms also have to be digested in order to maintain health in life. When you learn how to eliminate negative patterns in the mind, you can work to amplify the positive ones and grow your character into something that will enable you to be both fulfilled and healthy. *We will look at a specific technique for this in chapter 6 called "Pranayama Technique for Dissipating Negative Energy."*

A fun way to test your own mind is to write down three healing modalities you want to try and three you don't on a piece of paper. This list could include things like cleansing your body with saltwater, aromatherapy, or a pranayama exercise to reduce stress, all of which will be discussed in the techniques section. (We will discuss modalities in more detail in part 2). Write down your feelings about each modality, then go out and do all of them. This may take some time to give them all a fair chance, as each will require consistency in their pursuit. Once you've tried these different modalities and given them all a fair chance, go back and reassess your feelings about them. I guarantee that you will surprise yourself and learn why it is so important to listen to the heart and not the mind!

Experimenting with different modalities and approaches toward healing will be beneficial in overriding the impressions stored in the mind and also in helping you discover what and who you really are, beyond the mind. It's the way the mind processes information that leads to the rest of the emotional and physical problems. Learning to listen to the feelings, the heart, intuition, and subtle awareness will all help in the healing process and make any modality more effective. (*We will discuss feelings and the heart in this chapter and learn a "Technique for Cultivating Intuition and Subtle Awareness" in chapter 6*). It will make it easier to let go of what the mind says and actively pursue things to bring healing to the mind, emotions, and body.

Why Such Emphasis on the Mind & Intellect?

You may be wondering why there is such emphasis on the mind in a book about health and healing. Mind forms one aspect of the mind, body, soul triad to being balanced and whole. It is also where energy starts to accumulate and stagnate before disease enters the body. Disease always starts internally. You don't catch cancer, chronic illness, or an autoimmune disease from someone. You may pick up bacteria or viruses from someone else, but only if you are susceptible to its specific energetic frequency. If the body, mind, and soul are in balance and working harmoniously, external stimuli don't settle into the body as disease or infections.

This state of balance has a lot to do with people who get sick frequently versus people who don't. This is the piece that Western medicine does not fully understand. It is also a piece that cannot be quantified, because everyone is so unique and there is no way to tell how in balance a person really is. It's not apparent to the eye or outer perception. Just as the mind can condense experiences into thought forms, when energy is made to move freely, the mind is also capable of great things beyond the scope of what science can understand. How is it that some people have photographic memories? How can some people quickly get the things they want and ask for in life? How is it that some people have the ability to heal extraordinarily quickly? These are all examples of what the mind can help accomplish when used to its highest potential.

Because Western medicine does not understand entirely how the brain functions or what a burden thought forms cause, it's also not understood how much mental sickness permeates our culture. I say "mental sickness" to distinguish from what we call mental illness. From a vibrational and energetic perspective, everyone has some degree of mental sickness. People who are categorized as mentally ill have merely gotten to a point where they can no longer control a certain aspect of their mind. This is an unfortunate (and sad, from my perspective) way of perceiving the mind. People with acknowledged mental illnesses such as schizophrenia, depression, or bipolar disorder are ostracized and drugged but not really helped. Drugs don't get rid of the burden in the mind; they work to anesthetize or suppress it, merely covering up the symptoms that manifest as a result of the imbalances present. It's like throwing a rug over a pile of trash and pretending it doesn't exist. You can hide it for a while, but eventually everything that is covered up will meet the light of day.

If you don't control the mind, the thought forms you put in it will control you. You can use the mind to cultivate your character to do absolutely great things or you can let it control you and make you a monster. Who doesn't want to be in control of every single one of their decisions? Is there anyone alive that would voluntarily choose to be reactive to life or succumb to uncontrollable urges rather than learn how to be always confident and in control of their thoughts and desires? I don't think so. I don't think anyone wants to be out of control of their body or life; people become out of control because they don't know other ways to cope with their inner burden.

The Positive Aspects of the Mind

Let's now look at the highly beneficial aspects of the mind and how it can be used as a very powerful tool to facilitate balance in all areas of life. So far, we've looked at thought forms that happen spontaneously as a result of life's occurrences. It's quite possible to create positive thought forms and tendencies that will steer life in a very beneficial direction. If you don't want life to be controlled by external situations and experiences, you have to create the experiences in your life that will shape the way you think about and perceive the world.

Whatever a person does consistently (as in each and every day) will become a natural part of life. Over time, the impression becomes a habit and you'll keep up with the routine without effort. Meditation and affirmation are good examples of a beneficial daily routine to cultivate. You can find some meditation and affirmation techniques to practice in chapter 6. It's not that these things alone will change life instantly, but because of the power of the mind and how the mind relates to the experience, people who consistently meditate and focus on positive affirmations every single day form the habit of becoming positive. It's that simple. The mind is really a very simple thing, but working with it and bringing it under your conscious control takes impeccable discipline, effort, and consistency. You can definitely reap the positive things the mind has to offer if you cultivate strong willpower and a consistent daily practice of working with it. Practicing the techniques given in chapter 6 will all work on some aspect of the mind.

You'll become whatever you focus on, so learn to control your mind. If you focus on cultivating character and doing things that steer your life in the direction you want to go, the consistency in effort will in time override the latent impressions stored in the mind. The positive momentum will sustain itself and make it easier to do more and more things that bring happiness, clarity, and overall well-being to life.

The Heart's Role in Healing

The consequence of denying the need for love and fullness results in a state of inner poverty. This has extremely practical implications to life and health. Before we get into the topic of inner poverty versus inner prosperity, let's define the heart so we know exactly what we're dealing with. What exactly is the heart? This is the mystery of all mysteries in life. The heart is to be experienced and lived; not understood! It's the deepest part of you, all of your dreams, true desires, and aspirations.

Physically, the heart is the organ that holds everything together and sustains the rest of the body. The heart pumps oxygenated blood to the entire body through the circulatory system. Oxygen-depleted blood is returned to the heart, where it is then pumped to the lungs to dump carbon dioxide and absorb oxygen. Oxygen-rich blood then returns to the heart and is pumped through the rest of the body. This cycle is never ending, until a person dies. The heart brings nourishment to every part of the body and is always working nonstop. While a person can survive for a while in a brain-dead or comatose state, a person cannot survive if the heart stops beating.

Spiritually, the heart is the seat of the soul. The soul is considered to be the portion of you that is intrinsically connected to God. The soul is the microcosmic portion of the macrocosmic Godhead—the All That Is. The soul carries with it an innate intelligence of each of our individual life's purpose. It contains all experiences and all desires, constituting the fundamental basis for everything that a person is. The physical constitution, psychological temperament, and innate life purpose (also called *dharma*) come from the subtle essence of the heart. From purpose comes the structure of everything else: constitution, temperament, and personality. The heart holds everything together and works to keep life in balance, nourishing all of life with the essence of God and the deepest part of a person's core self. Note that I am not referring to God as some being sitting off in the sky, but the intrinsic fabric of everything a person is.

Feelings are a form of the heart's communication.
What feeling you get from an experience is solely
dependent on which aspect of you is most in control
(is it the mind or the heart?) and how well the mind
and the heart get along. Do your mind and heart
fight with each other? Do you even know what your
heart thinks about something? When there is conflict
between mind and heart, feelings will be turbulent.
When a person's feelings are very strong and still go
against the mind, problems occur in life: emotional
outbursts, lack of stability, doubt in oneself, fear, and
all of the other experiences that drive us farther and
farther away from the innate knowing of the heart.
Thoughts can be understood as the surface expression
of the heart whereas feelings represent the depth of
the heart. Mind and heart are not really separate, so
when they don't function as a cohesive whole, it is the
root cause of many of life's problems.

Feelings hold valuable keys to our life
purpose. You can look to them as a way of deeply
understanding the fundamental essence you carry
and also as a way of understanding what is going
on in the conscious and subconscious minds. If
you know your heart well enough and know what
your overall life purpose is, it is entirely possible
to tease out of feelings what portions are coming
from the conditioned mind. Feelings are a gateway
for healing the mind because they expose what is

really going on in the mind. Sometimes, it's not possible to see or understand this all for ourselves. Getting an outside perspective from a counselor, therapist, or spiritual guide is an excellent way to gain clarity so you can more quickly and accurately figure out what is really going on inside of you.

Emotionally, the heart is considered the seat of love itself. We as humans feel fullness and unification as love. It's a unique vibration that emanates from someone who feels full and complete. All expressions and shades of love come from this root essence. Love is the one area of life that cannot be denied and anyone who has been in love or felt love itself will tell you it is a force intrinsically more powerful than anything else in existence. When we try to deny the need for love, we deny the necessity of our own completeness and fullness, which leads to an unbalanced state of living resulting in inner poverty.

Inner Poverty vs. Inner Prosperity

I still remember the very first time my family celebrated Valentine's Day when I was a young child. Upon learning there was an entire day dedicated solely to the purpose of spreading and feeling love, my heart overflowed with such delight and joy! To this day, I remember how that moment made me feel: the thought of this memory makes me smile every time, no matter how I feel in the moment. That feeling of overwhelming joy is how I would describe what inner prosperity is like.

It's important to grasp what inner poverty and inner prosperity really mean. The experiences for each of us are different, but the underlying energy is the same. Inner prosperity is the inner stability and fullness we experience when the heart's dreams (which emanate directly from the soul) are given the focus and nourishment needed to grow. Feeling intrinsically good about oneself inwardly has nothing to do with outer reality; it comes from feeling inwardly prosperous. Happiness, creative energy, and feelings of self-worth cannot be experienced consistently without the fuel of inner prosperity. It's the nourishing energy of inner prosperity that sustains both happiness and all forms of health and well-being. Inner prosperity is the fuel for accomplishing all things whereas inner poverty reflects the lack of this nourishing and sustaining life energy.

Inner poverty is a direct result of not living one's life based on the fabric of the heart and soul, of which the temperament, constitution, and character are all manifestations. When this inner, innate nature of a person is disregarded, no matter what comes in life externally, it will not lead to fulfillment inwardly. In fact, it often leads to greater and greater discontent and a lack of understanding of why nothing in life seems meaningful. Earlier I said that people can't deny love. Don't misunderstand; people do deny love all the time, but in doing so there are consequences—just as there are consequences to any form of imbalance.

Feelings of inner prosperity are the most important subtle energy to cultivate for success in healing and maintaining well-being. Inner prosperity is directly connected to feelings of self-worth and what a person feels they are capable of achieving in life. If a person does not feel like they can achieve anything good, they won't try. If a person does not have a consistent and sustaining inner positive energy to help them accomplish goals, the pursuit will end before the goal is reached due to lack of momentum. It does not matter what the goal is—it could be getting a new job or it could be learning to heal from an illness or major life change. No matter what the goal, all good things and the ability to attain successful results come from cultivating inner prosperity.

People suffering from inner poverty display a few telltale signs and symptoms, which are important to recognize both in oneself and in the pursuit of helping to heal others. Symptoms of inner poverty include becoming a workaholic, having an overemphasis on intellectualism at the expense of dreams and feelings, a need for rational left-brained thought to make decisions, and at its most extreme, the inclination to act violently toward either humans or animals. Some things in life are very simple; if you are happy, you won't ever want to harm others. You'll want to help them be happy too! If you are fulfilled inwardly, there is no need for defense mechanisms that negate the importance of feelings.

Even some very good-hearted people exhibit signs of inner poverty, but in a very opposite way. They are constantly giving to others and doing charitable work, but never adequately taking care of themselves. These people recognize the fundamental truth that giving is the best way of getting what is needed, but have not learned how to adequately receive and fill themselves with positive feelings and self-worth. Charity and compassion must first start within oneself for it to be productive and rewarding, otherwise it might just be a means of escapism.

Regardless of how inner poverty manifests externally, the result is the same. No amount of outer abundance, material resources, or even love from other people can fill the void a person feels within themselves. The void begins when an individual loses sight of his or her innate being and life's calling, when the words of others and the thoughts of the mind overshadow the intrinsic being of the heart. Really, you are the greatest gift you will ever receive! Your entire constitution was created based on your core purpose in life, so intrinsically, each and every person already has all of the tools they need within them to be successful, prosperous, happy, and healthy in life. Find that happy place within yourself if you ever lose touch of your feelings of prosperity. For me, it is the remembrance of my first Valentine's Day. What is it for you?

The basis of the heart is for people to live happy, fulfilling lives. There is boundless energy that comes from the heart when it is allowed to express itself freely. The heart holds all of the secrets we need to be happy and fulfilled. Use your feelings for a greater means of discovery if you are uncertain of what the heart is trying to say. Seek assistance from others when needed. Use all of the resources at your disposal. Don't expect to know everything yourself—the heart knows everything, but it takes practice at discerning its voice from that of the mind and preconditioned reactions to life.

The mind can be trained to be one of the most powerful healing tools in existence. When the mind works with the heart and not against it, the combined momentum can accomplish nearly anything. When you work from the heart and the depth of the soul, there is boundless energy to get things done. When work comes from the mind and goes against the natural flow of a person's dharma, tiredness and fatigue ensue quickly. Have you noticed this in your own life? When you do what you love, how effortless does the endeavor seem? What about when you do things you hate or feel you have to do just to survive? Anything written in this book is meant to be delved into and experienced—it's not theoretical knowledge. Try this for yourself and note the results. I bet you'll find, to no surprise, when you are truly joyous and happy how time flies and energy is there.

Inner Prosperity,
Affirmation & Abundance

There has been a lot of talk the past few years about the secrets of abundance, positivity, and gratitude's role in successful living. Both feeling positive about oneself and cultivating gratitude in life come from inner prosperity. They are natural reflections of living a heart-centered life. Many people have heard that one way to cultivate positivity in life is through affirmation, which are positive statements you make about yourself that you believe or deeply want to believe. For example, saying, "I am beautiful" every day helps to align both mind and feelings with the vibration of beauty. However, a person who is inwardly poor will not be able to authentically have gratitude or positive feelings about life, and as such, no amount of affirmation will make it so. The phrase, "You reap what you sow," has a very deep meaning in this; you can only get in life what you really are and what you really inwardly know and feel to be true, not what you want to be true.

Using affirmations to help manifest the things you want in life works best when there is an established foundation of inner prosperity. Otherwise, the affirmation is going directly against what is felt inside and creates tension. Time and persistence can help in lessening this tension, but in the short term, using an affirmation you don't really believe may do more harm than good. If a person holds deeply ingrained notions that prevent inner prosperity and happiness, it will take a lot of work and consistent effort to move past this. Prosperity, inner or outer, is an energy that flows. Anything that acts to obstruct this free-flowing energy will limit its ability to be felt and experienced.

Mantra, on the other hand, has beneficial results for everyone and can be used to dissolve feelings that prevent or somehow limit inner prosperity. The seed sounds found in mantra work directly within and upon the subtle body; this concept will be discussed later.

The main lesson in inner prosperity is to work with what you have and not to focus on how small or large your feelings of prosperity are. Work with it, nourish it, and it will grow. It's technically impossible to work with something you don't have, yet this is what the mind tries to convince us to do. As opposed to focusing on the positives we have in life and working to nourish them, the mind puts attention on the negatives and things we don't have, and then inner prosperity dwindles.

It's human nature to look at a bad situation in life and try to focus on something opposite as a means of escapism rather than to setting realistic goals to attain success. Here's an example. If a person is extremely unhealthy, simply repeatedly telling themselves, "I am healthy," does not make them healthy. If affirmation is used in this way, it does not work because it goes against what both the mind and heart know to be true. If affirmation is used in conjunction with inner prosperity and a person's life purpose, and is tempered with realistic goals that are in proportion to the amount of inner prosperity you feel, success will be a natural result. For example, if this same unhealthy person knows he is unhealthy and takes appropriate measures to facilitate health being brought into balance while telling himself, "I am working toward health and well-being," the affirmation is truthful and will contribute to building positive momentum that over time will lead to stability in this pursuit.

Whenever an affirmation works in alignment with the depth of the heart's knowing, momentum is built toward cultivating inner prosperity. However, the biggest challenge people face is eliminating all of the garbage and conditioned thoughts of the mind that act to prevent inner prosperity. Through working intently to clear out the conditioned thought forms in the mind simultaneously with honoring the inner abode and dreams of the heart, progress toward balanced prosperity, inner and outer, can be achieved.

We will continue to explore different temperament types, body constitutions, and how to identify what they all mean and how to work with and heal their vibrational energies so that you can cultivate in yourself the best possible person you can be. Understanding some basics about the mind and heart's role in healing will set a solid foundation for learning what types of techniques work best for you. Regardless of what techniques you use, the secret to success comes from the foundation in understanding both your mind and heart.

TWO

All About the Energy Body

· · · · · · · · · · · · · ·

So far we've taken a basic look at vibrational healing and how it is connected to the mind, intellect, heart, and feelings. These four components deal directly with the mind and soul aspects of the mind, body, soul triad and directly impact what happens in the physical body. They are indispensable parts of life and health, so to better understand them and how they work will bring great depth to your journey in healing. In this chapter, we will discuss what subtle energy is, the different places it comes from, and how to cultivate it within one's self. We will also take a look at the subtle energy body and each of the seven main chakras, plus three more of great importance to health and healing. From there, it becomes possible to understand the basics of individual temperament and physical constitution, which we will discuss in terms of the gunas and elements of nature.

Subtle Energy—What is It?

What is it that gives people their own unique appearance, moods, talents, and desires? What makes each person a unique individual? It comes down to the inner disposition and subtle building blocks of life, which includes subtle energy known as prana or chi, and the subtle body, which consists of the chakras, the gunas, and the five elements. Let's start by looking at subtle energy itself, what it is, what it isn't, and how it can be conceptualized.

Have you experienced subtle energy? Have you felt the whirling of your chakras or tingling in your hands after you rub them together? Have you ever had an energy-healing session that left you feeling like things inside of you were moving, but you couldn't describe what it was? I've felt energy to some degree since I was young, but one of the earliest and most notable experiences of it for me was when I was taken to see an acupuncturist. How they could place these thin needles just barely in the skin and make my whole body vibrate was fascinating to me! It definitely got me hooked on thinking outside of the conventional box regarding health and healing. As a child I had no idea what a chakra was or what subtle energy was; I just knew something was happening inside of me that was awesome and unique.

In my early twenties, I decided to learn more about subtle energy and the unseen aspects of life to deepen my understanding of life. I'll sum it up in a practical and informational way to start you on your exploration. The basis of the subtle body is a system of interconnecting subtle energy channels that make up the rest of your being, both subtle and physical. These channels, or conduits of subtle energy, are commonly referred to as meridians or nadis. The Vedas, one of the primary spiritual scriptures of India, say there are 72,000 different nadis (similar to nerves) in the body. Nadis work together as channels to move subtle energy through the entire body and are also the conduits that form what we refer to as chakras.

Subtle energy is the innate life force we all have. It can be thought of as vitality, motivation, drive, and any number of other common conceptions. It's the subtle force that drives all other aspects of being—innate biological processes, the body's ability to heal, a person's charisma—and is the fuel we use to live our dreams. Subtle energy is commonly referred to as chi, qi, or prana; *chi* and *qi* being its Chinese words, and *prana* the Sanskrit word. I am defining these now so when you read and hear these words elsewhere, you'll know they all refer to the same underlying energy.

A common question about subtle energy is in its relation to kundalini. Kundalini is definitely subtle energy, but not all subtle energy is kundalini. There are many differing opinions about what the differences are between subtle energy and kundalini itself. People have different experiences based on their own predisposition, temperament, spiritual or religious tradition, character, and core desires, making it impossible to give kundalini one single definition; no two people will experience kundalini, or subtle energy, in exactly the same ways. For the sake of conceptualization and inner discernment, the most notable difference is the source; subtle energy can be cultivated in numerous ways, both internal and external, whereas kundalini only comes from within the deepest part of one's own being. Also, tangible differences are felt on an experiential level between the two, but the differences mostly come down to the intensity of experiences, as the manifestations of both can overlap. To repeat, kundalini is definitely subtle energy, but not all subtle energy is kundalini. While subtle energy and kundalini utilize the same energy, kundalini has the always interconnected consciousness of the Soul as the primary directing force and substance behind how subtle energy moves and where it is derived from. You can think of kundalini as the Soul itself and how the Soul moves its unified consciousness through the body. The Soul as the spark of God and self, the microcosmic form of the macrocosmic universe, already contains everything inside of it as part of it. As such, it needs no other source to derive its energy. Kundalini can be very intense in its experience because it is a pure, raw form of power that is incomparable to anything else. For some people, the intensity is amazing—joyful and blissful! For others, it can be quite painful, invoking tremendous fears and actual physical illnesses. It all depends on what is stored within the subtle body.

Not all subtle bodies are created equal, as is seen when people face problems with kundalini energy. In practical terms, every person has the same components, the same nadi conduits, chakras, and overall subtle body system, but how well the system functions is unique to each and every individual. The subtle body can be strong and robust, or weak and fragile. It can be strengthened through applied practice or weakened through neglect and improper care of oneself. It can also get mucked up over time and develop blockages that prevent energy from flowing freely through parts of it. To be in optimum emotional, physical, and spiritual heath, the subtle body must be kept strong and in good condition. A strong subtle body is required for people seeking to cultivate either psychic or healing abilities.

Think of the subtle body as a lightbulb and subtle energy as the electricity that goes to the lightbulb. If a lightbulb is only capable of containing 60 watts of electricity and a person tries to put 200 watts through it, the current will destroy the lightbulb. With no lightbulb, electricity has no conduit to express itself and shine light. Trying to understand and work with subtle energy through a weak subtle body is like trying to put 200 watts of electricity through a 60-watt bulb; it doesn't work and can lead to problems. When a person's subtle body is mucked up with blockages another way to think of it is like a sink that is backed up; the pipes need to be cleaned out before water can flow freely through. Both electricity and water are good analogies for how subtle energy flows in the subtle body, as there are different expressions of subtle energy! Subtle energy can take on different characteristics based on a person's intentions, focus, and willpower. It will also express itself differently in different parts of the mind, body, soul system. Sometimes it's gentle and cooling and at other times, hot, fiery, and electric!

Subtle energy can be given different names based on where it is residing in the body and what it is doing, but when it comes down to it, it's all the same core substance. Let's use sunlight for an example. Sunlight contains in it the visible spectrum of the rainbow, although we don't see these distinct colors or frequencies of their own accord when they are combined together in the form of sunlight. Subtle energy also contains many different frequencies of energies in it that combine to form a unified whole subtle energy current. Through perception and intention, energy becomes distinct frequencies (just like the distinct rays of the sun) and takes on its own unique personality. This will become clearer as we look at the chakras and the different energy sources they contain.

A Look at Chakras

Chakras are focal points of energy in our bodies that occur as a result of a convergence of subtle energy. The nadis of the subtle body carry subtle energy from one place to another, intersecting with one another and forming a complex network of conduits that take energy everywhere in the body. The major intersecting points for nadis are chakras. Any place in the body where you have numerous, perhaps thousands of intersecting energy points is going to be a powerful place that affects all level of being including mind, body, emotions, and soul. Technically the soul itself is impenetrable and always remains the same, but our perceptions of it, access to it, and ability for it to work in harmony with the rest of the mind, body, and emotions are affected by how energy moves in the subtle body system, and the chakras in particular.

There are literally hundreds of books out there that talk about the structure of the chakras, mantras, and everything you could possibly want to know, so here I'm going to discuss only the basics of the structure (for purposes of visualization) and talk much more in depth about the consciousness and temperament that goes into each of these energy centers in the body. Each chakra is unique, and when they act together make a whole unified person. When chakras are not in harmony, are not balanced, or contain blockages that prevent energy from flowing freely through them, a person's moods, temperament, behavior, and even physical health can be affected.

Chakras have been described as looking like a lotus flower, each with a distinct number of petals. The petals of the chakras represent the different abilities of the mind, or brain centers, and are also known as dalas. The analogy of a flower is nice, as it invokes a sense of beauty and wonder that is essential for cultivating the inner prosperity we previously discussed. Each petal contained in a chakra is a focal point for a unique energy. The first six main chakras in the body have a total of fifty combined petals—fifty unique energy emanations. These fifty petals are repeated twenty times each in the crown chakra, to give the thousand-petaled lotus of the crown chakra. The crown chakra contains the same dalas found in the first six chakras, but functions from a place of these energies coming together in harmony where they all work together, as part of the whole. Each of the twenty repetitions of the dalas increases in energy frequency, magnifying their potency in the crown chakra. The fact that the crown chakra, often seen as the abode of enlightenment, contains nothing unique but the same energies found in the main chakras of the subtle body system, working together in one whole mechanism, hints further at the unity of everything we are and contain. The crown chakra cannot become fully functional, open, and receptive until everything it contains (which is everything else inside of us) is functioning from a place of unity and harmony.

All chakras have mantras or sound current vibrational frequencies that correspond with their energies. The first five chakras also have corresponding elements that relate to our sensory perceptions of life. I'll focus on concepts dealing with each chakra that are not widely discussed, yet are crucial to health, well-being, and understanding who each of us really is.

Many people don't directly experience their subtle bodies. Subtle energy as a whole is something that people need to learn to cultivate and work with—having an intellectual understanding is just not enough. Talking about complex chakra concepts that only spiritual adepts with extensive meditation or spiritual practice will experience excludes many people who are simply seeking to connect with themselves. And while I can outline a lot of information on the chakras, unless a person experiences this directly and knows how to work with the subtle energy, it won't do much good.

A useful way for any person to start understanding subtle energy is by learning about their own guna (sattva, rajas, and tamas) and elemental composition (earth, air, fire, water, and ether) through direct experience. Guna in this context relates directly to individual temperament or character, whereas elemental composition relates to both lifestyle tendencies and physical body composition. Having the direct experience of these happens when you are able to consciously identify which gunas or elements are the most powerful in your life at a given time. Once the direct experience of temperament or body composition is awakened, a person can move in the direction recommended to deepen an integrated learning process. By taking the time to learn and explore your own temperament, you can learn to discern what makes you "you"; this integrated learning process gives rise to the awareness of inner knowing, which in and of itself works to eliminate false knowledge.

Here is a personal example. I like activity and excitement, but I also have a deep love of home and hearth. My intellect feeds itself on contemplation and inquiry. I like good food and company, in moderation. I like solitude, in moderation. I like nature and winter and the sound of flowing water. I love fragrances and the basic passions of life. I love music, singing, and dance. I am flexible and listen, but when I set my mind to a course of action, I follow through to the very end with pinpoint focus and devotion. I value sacredness above all else. Through knowing all of this about myself and from several years of contemplation and learning, I was able to discern I'm a very earth-, fire-, and ether-based person, both in psychological temperament as it relates to the gunas and also in bodily composition and tendencies as they relate to the elements. These attributes will be explained in greater detail when we learn about the gunas and the elements in chapter 3.

Let's explore the chakras as they relate to temperament and composition. By understanding even the basics of your own temperament, you can effectively work with the energy in each chakra to bring about balance, inner prosperity, and vibrancy in life.

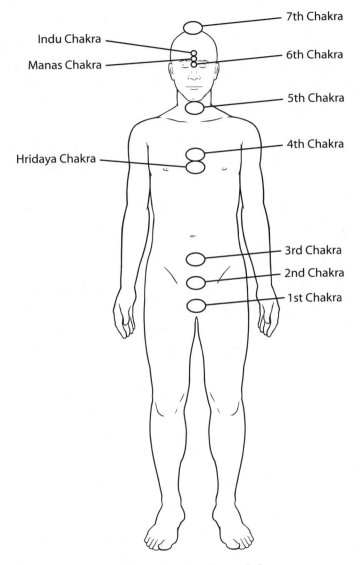

7th Chakra

Indu Chakra

6th Chakra

Manas Chakra

5th Chakra

4th Chakra

Hridaya Chakra

3rd Chakra

2nd Chakra

1st Chakra

Figure showing the ten chakras.

First Chakra (Muladhara)—
Root Foundations

The first chakra in the body is found near the base of the spine in the genital region. It is referred to as the first chakra, root chakra, or by its name Muladhara. *Muladhara* means "root support" and that is exactly what this chakra energy provides people. It provides the foundation of all aspects of life. It's considered the seat of the soul, the kundalini, and the place to build foundations from. In order for anything built in life to be stable, whether it's a house or an idea, it must have a solid foundation. With no foundation, what can be built? With a rickety foundation, everything built on top of it will be no more stable than a house of cards. The solidarity of this chakra is further supported by its corresponding element, which is earth.

The petals on this chakra relate to the primal passions of life. If these passions are lacking, they will be expressed as needs; if these passions are present and integrated into an overall healthy lifestyle, they will be experienced as joy and even bliss. Primal passions of life include food, because a lot of the subtle energy necessary for survival comes from food; sex, because sex is relaxing and procreation is necessary for survival of the human species; sleep, because sleep is required for healing and integration; and lastly peace, because peace is essential to feeling connected with universe. A person cannot feel the complete connection with the soul or the universe without an underlying sense of peace that lays doubt and discord to rest. This type of peace does not mean being peaceful in disposition or character, but feeling completely secure in life and what it brings. It's this deep-seated peace that gives rise to the most dynamic and fearless people in the world.

While life brings about many shades of gray, complexities to situations and perceptions, the way we relate to ourselves in our most fundamental passions and root chakra energy needs to be as black and white as possible. Ambiguity in perceptions is not acceptable when it comes to building strong foundations in life. The earth element corresponds with the root chakra and is also solid and fixed, but is a fertile place for growth. Since this chakra is about foundations and the root support for all life, it is considered the seat of a person's unique life path and personal calling, also known as dharma. If dharma is not lived and nourished from the root chakra, it cannot grow and develop anywhere else in the subtle body or in life.

In order to get energy flowing freely in the root chakra, there has to be a balance between basic biological urges and life purpose. When there is balance in these very primal expressions and a person learns how to control these expressions, making them work together instead of against each other, the root chakra energy can function in a whole and complete manner. I like to think of this as "Life 101." Too much sleep leads to inertia and sloth; too little leads to overload and depletion. Too much food leads to obesity and an unhealthy body and too little leaves a person without needed energy, and so on. Too much or too little sex is dependent on a variety of other issues that can't be easily discussed. Peace cannot be experienced until these other three (the relationship to sleep, food, and sexuality) are in balance.

Because of the first chakra's connection to dharma and overall life path, to strong foundations, and to the powerful soul energy itself, it is also seen as the place within that either creates or removes obstacles in life. While it would be great to be very solid and well-defined in this chakra from day one, life does not always happen that way. Cultivating this sort of strong foundation takes time and inner work to understand what is needed and to cultivate the confidence required to live life in pursuit of your unique life's calling. The first chakra is both a starting point for setting clear intentions and healthy habits and is also an ending point. One of the last things to be achieved through mind, body, soul balance is the strong foundation that will support everything in life, unequivocally, in all situations. When the first chakra becomes a means of support without expending considerable energy to keep it balanced and well-conditioned, life can take on any dimensions a person is willing to work for.

Temperament- (guna) based modalities as will be outlined in chapter 6 are good starting points for working with the first chakra's energy. It is temperament and overall life path which give rise to powerful and balanced energy in the first chakra. *In chapter 6 you will also find a "Technique for Cultivating Inner Prosperity," which will help set a solid foundation and platform to grow from in the first chakra.*

Second Chakra (Svadhisthana)—
The Abode of Self

The second chakra in the body is found above the genital region in the lower abdomen below the navel center. It is known as the *Svadhisthana* chakra, which means "abode of self." While the soul itself is not seated in the second chakra, for a number of reasons the way in which we perceive it and life is. Everything that exists is always seen through the lens of perception, so the perceptions a person has must be clear in order to be balanced, healthy, and fulfilled. Perceptions come both from feelings and from mind, as was discussed previously. Mind is influenced by thought forms and sensory contact from smell, taste, sight, touch, and sound, which have direct correlations to the elements. The second chakra is unique in that it holds the vibrations of all of the elements except ether inside of it, as a way to teach us how to feel about life and experience.

The second chakra also relates to the concepts of purity of self and the intrinsic strength that comes from purity. Purity is a concept that relates specifically to the individual in question, not a uniform notion of something as pure or impure. It's about how you relate to the unique aspects of yourself, your unique elemental composition, your dharma, your temperament, and your combined life's experiences. If any of these pieces are not being related to properly, energetic blockages will be found in the second chakra. If experiences and sensory impressions in life have caused a person to disconnect from their inner self, this will be reflected through blockages in this chakra's energy. The second chakra also strongly relates to the capacity to flow because of its connection to water element.

To better understand what I mean by the concept of purity of self, think about a small child or baby. Babies cry when they are unhappy or need something and laugh when they are happy. Children say exactly what they mean ("I want ice cream now!") without a second thought. It's a totally pure and unbiased expression of what is felt without being filtered through the mind. That is what is meant by purity of self; no filters on authentic expression. Children are not embarrassed by situations until they are taught to be. Children feel no shame until they learn it from someone else. This means that children are always in the present moment and are not affected by thought forms found in the mind. As such, they are purely themselves and only function from the heart, with no mind or reason involved. This is difficult for adults because of the learned patterns and conditioning of the mind we all face; it's the mind's conditioning that contaminates a person's perceptions of life and purity of self.

When the mind and thought forms get involved, they shift perceptions of self and the ways in which a person relates to their innate nature and dharma. Because of this connection between perception and thought forms, the second chakra is considered the seat of the subconscious mind. Perceptions are reflections of our cumulative life experiences. One of the great powers the second chakra provides us is the ability to be flexible, to integrate new things into our own reality so that we may become what we want to become.

Strength and purity of self are intrinsically interconnected because, when given proper nourishment, what is purely itself will grow to be strong and robust with time. If you nourish the root essence of yourself, you will grow. However, if you nourish false perceptions of yourself, those false perceptions will grow. Your life is a garden of being and perceptions; if you don't get rid of the weeds, they will grow alongside your flowers, obscuring their beauty. To make a garden strong, the weeds must be pulled so that the flowers get all the nutrients and attention they need to thrive. To grow into yourself, the weeds of false perceptions must be pulled out so as to not obstruct the flow and who you really are. Strength is required to eliminate everything that would try to keep you from being your own self, so to be purely yourself, you must also have strength.

Because of the connection to its flowing nature, water, and receptivity to what we experience in life, the second chakra is an important place to establish very healthy, clear boundaries of self. Boundaries are the strength aspect of the second chakra, which is essential for maintaining clear perceptions of yourself. Having a lack of appropriate boundaries means the thoughts and feelings of other people can easily flow into you and change your own feelings and perceptions of life. When second chakra boundaries are not strong and your feelings mix with other people's feelings and perceptions, it becomes difficult to know who you truly are and what you really believe. Individuality and a clear sense of dharma comes from having healthy boundaries. Boundaries create your individual vehicle of mind and body, how they relate to the experiences of life and how the soul perceives it all. How capable do you feel of knowing and living your dharma? Do you have a clear sense of your life's purpose, your likes, your dislikes, and your desires, or do these feelings fluctuate depending on what you are doing or who you are spending time with? If you find your feelings and perceptions frequently change or are unclear, it is because the second chakra's energy needs to be further developed and robust boundaries of self need to be established. Negative experiences in life, pain, and violence affect this chakra and require a lot of healing and nurturance to correct. Do you feel victimized or like an open canvas to create your reality as you see fit?

The flowing nature of the second chakra lies in its creative energies. We can all create our realities by learning the cycles and energies of creativity, preservation, and destruction. All healing comes from the ability to change; either to move a hurt area toward being whole by creating and sustaining a nourishing energy, or to destroy some negative manifestation that obscures well-being. Both require fluidity, change, and connection to the root essence of self. Let go of the old and painful and welcome the whole and nurturing. Since life will never be all good experiences, the ability to flow and shift perceptions gives the ability to take the good from any situation and easily discard the bad. Inclination toward sadness and worry reflect a weakened second chakra and show where we need to learn to flow and bring inner prosperity into our being.

We discussed the primal passions of life as they are connected with the first chakra. The second chakra is where these passions take on an individual shape and form based on life experience. The passions of life combined with temperament and body composition (the gunas and elements that will be discussed in chapter 3) and an individual's life experiences shape what a person becomes. The flowing nature of the second chakra helps us heal, change, grow, and effectively deal with all aspects of life. Solid boundaries help us to clearly know who we are and how to keep out feelings that are not in our best interests. The combination of boundaries and a flowing nature provides an excellent balance to take all of life's experiences and use them in a positive way to determine what we want and shape our life's calling.

Chapter 6 outlines techniques and methods for working with water element, which will be highly beneficial for working with the second chakra's energy, such as "Water Element Cleansing Technique."

Third Chakra (Manipura)— The City of Jewels

The third chakra is located right at the level of the navel point. It is known as *Manipura*, which means "city of jewels" in Sanskrit. It is the seat of fire element, willpower, personal empowerment, and desire. It is also connected to the sense perception of sight. As the chakra with perhaps the densest concentration of subtle energy, it directs prana (life force) into other areas of the body and brings needed subtle energy nourishment to the entire body. People with strong charisma usually have a very robust third chakra. Adept healers know how to use and direct this energy in their practice and also use it to keep themselves healthy, positive, and well-balanced.

Have you ever felt nauseous or unsettled in your stomach after someone has said or done something to make you feel bad? This comes because your sense of power and control of yourself has been affected in the third chakra. Whatever you desire in life, the third chakra brings it into fruition. This is where what's going on in a person's subtle energies start to become noticeable in the physical world. This chakra's energy gives proof if your life is working for you or not. Successful people know how to use their focused willpower and desires to bring fuel to everything in life they want to create. When subtle energy fuels intention, things happen and desires are manifested. Unsuccessful people are scattered in their pursuits or are unclear about what their desires really are. When there are too many desires, none of them get the full intention and focus necessary to make them a reality.

What a person desires in life will intrinsically come from how balanced they are and how well developed the sense of self is, as we discussed with the second chakra. When these energies are all working and flowing properly, desire will align itself naturally with a person's highest potential and dharma. When there are fears or other negative emotions, dharmic pursuit gets sidetracked and a person's pranic energy gets focused on other less important desires. The three main constrictions in the first three chakras are greed, lust, and selfish desire, respectively. When any or all of these three consume a person's thoughts, energy will go toward their fruition and not toward fulfilling one's life purpose.

When desires of any kind are blocked, anger develops. Angry people always have some sort of blockage in the third chakra. Fear is another negative trait harbored in the third chakra that acts to constrict fulfillment on any level. The first three chakras are where you will find the most energy blockages because these are the three chakras that directly affect how people relate to themselves and the world at large. These are major life lessons and can take a long time to work out. When the third chakra is functioning properly, people are positive, upbeat, charismatic, natural leaders. Perceptions of inward negativity are so small that they are easily hidden by their positive perspective. People who have a well-developed third chakra will find they get what they want in life—even if these desires are not in their best interest. To ensure desires are in alignment with dharma, the first, second, and third chakra energies all need to be in balance and harmony.

The name Manipura, or city of jewels, alludes to the infinite potential that this energy center contains and may be used for reaping the highest successes in life with all desires being fulfilled. Everyone has difficulties in life; that is what makes it life. Successful people have difficulties too, and perhaps even more than the average person, but their success comes from how they relate to challenges. Any challenge can be overcome with the proper knowledge and actions, and perhaps even more importantly, the proper attitude of self-empowerment. When you feel empowered, you'll always find a way to overcome any difficulty. With such dense pranic energy, the third chakra is instrumental in all healing. By directing the flow of energy well, health for yourself and others is a very attainable result.

Working with techniques that relate to rajas guna and fire element will both work well for stimulating the third chakra; both are found in chapter 6. *The "Visualization for Cultivating Subtle Energy" technique is a good inner technique to start with.* If you practice yoga or other forms of physical fitness, techniques that focus directly on the abdominal area and the navel point will stimulate the third chakra's energy. Working through the body is a good way to work with this energy and really feel it on a physical level.

Fourth Chakra (Anahata)— The Unstruck Sound

The fourth chakra is known as the *Anahata* chakra, which means "unstruck sound" in Sanskrit and relates to the sense perception of touch. Many people think of this as the heart chakra, but it is not; we will discuss the *Hridaya* chakra (heart chakra) in detail later in this chapter. The Anahata chakra is the place in the subtle body where there is a convergence of energies, which leads to infinite possibility and the very real possibility of being completely in tune with both the external universe and your own inner universe. When both external and internal work together in harmony, there is infinite potential to create, express, and be fully in alignment with one's life purpose.

The fourth chakra is a focal point. It is where you will see, experience, and perceive the cumulative information of all the chakras below and above Anahata together. This energy center merges everything that you are into one and gives you the ability to perceive your full potential. The quiet voice of intuition comes from this chakra; when a person learns to work well with this energy, knowledge takes on a whole new meaning. Instead of memorizing and assimilating external information from books or people, knowledge happens as a spontaneous inner knowing.

True knowing is different from learning. Learning can help stimulate the inner knowing that we all have inside of us, but the deep inner knowing comes from a place of silence, stillness, and potential energy, which the fourth chakra represents. Anahata means unstruck sound; this is significant, because when sound is audible, it is a creative energy frequency that moves in a specific direction for a specific purpose. Unstruck sound refers to the potential that lies within. Potential energy is dormant and needs a catalyst to bring it out. Only when you can clearly perceive your potential in life can you take appropriate action to manifest that potential.

The deeper a person goes into this energy center, the deeper connected they become to both themselves and the universe as a whole. The more a person becomes connected to the infinite potential of the universe, the more innate gratitude, humility, and inner prosperity can develop from it. If the first three chakras are well taken care of, it is easier to bring the potential energy perceived here and develop it into a practical, tangible reality. To dive deeply into any energy center in the body (all of the chakras are just specific energy centers), one's thoughts, feelings, and entire consciousness have to learn to work with the particular energy frequency you want to go deeper into. Just like pearls are recovered from diving deep and searching for them (you won't find them floating on the surface of water), the inner knowledge derived from any chakra's energy also has to be deeply and intensely pursued to find its metaphorical pearls. *In chapter 6 you will find a technique called "Visualization for Grounding Energy," which will help cultivate the ability to sit silently with any energy center you want to cultivate. You will also learn a "Technique for Cultivating Intuition & Subtle Awareness" in chapter 6.* The benefit of diving deep into the energy of the fourth chakra is the spontaneous inner knowing and heightened intuition that arises as a result of this chakra's energy.

The chakras below the fourth chakra relate to experience and the external work. The chakras below the fourth chakra deal with how we relate to our body and emotions, how we relate to money, sexuality, other people, personal empowerment and the like. Above the fourth chakra is where we start to incorporate the lessons we have learned from life experience, integrating these into more subtle realms of perception, where it becomes possible to understand life's influence on thoughts, feelings and more. Since the fourth chakra is really only as strong as its pieces (aka, everything else we are and all other energy centers), it's important to live a balanced life with equal emphasis on the chakras above and below Anahata. Oftentimes when people decide to pursue spirituality, there is an overemphasis on meditation and cultivating the higher perceptory chakras and little to no emphasis on working with the first three. This unbalanced approach leads to many problems and a lack of ability to follow through externally on what has been perceived internally. When people live from their upper chakras, life stays merely as potential and never moves into the realm of experience in the material world. There is great danger in this, because being aware of something is very different than living it. Actions make a difference in our worlds and in the worlds of people around us, not our awareness.

The fourth chakra can be worked on directly through meditation, as meditation affects our awareness and helps to bring a calmness that allows for clearer perception.

Meditation, of course, benefits every chakra, but the Anahata is where much of the direct experience of it comes from. Since this chakra is a focal point for all of the other energies and is really the essence of what most people strive for in having clear perceptions of this world and the subtle realms, it is extra important to develop a balanced, integrated, spiritual, and lifestyle practice that works on mind, body, and soul together as one.

Fifth Chakra (Vishuddha)— The Purification Center

The fifth chakra is known as the *Vishuddha* chakra, which means "purification center" in Sanskrit, and its corresponding element is ether, which represents space. Its corresponding sensory perception is hearing. It is located in the neck region, just below where the vocal cords sit. The fifth chakra is the body's center of purification. It is tied to both speaking and hearing and is intrinsically tied to the sound current through the ether element. Sound and mantra are great purifying agents and represent a very powerful vibrational frequency that can bring about great healing.

There are great lessons to be learned from the consciousness contained in this chakra's energy. In life, we hear things every day. We speak things every day, unless of course there is a disability that prevents hearing or speaking. Both what we hear and what we speak affect consciousness, thoughts, and overall health. The fifth chakra can be thought of as a gateway to what we let into our consciousness from the external world and what we allow to come out of our consciousness into the external world.

The fifth chakra represents our ability to filter and purify the things we hear and say in life, so what is heard and spoken can have a positive effect on the emotions. A person with a robust fifth chakra can learn to no longer be sensitive to either praise or criticism from others inwardly, while simultaneously having the capacity to invoke positivity and healing in others through speech. This happens due to a purification of the inner emotional state, where others no longer have the ability to sway an individual's beliefs and feelings of self. When we find ourselves being sensitive to what others say about us or to us, we know that this chakra needs some work.

This chakra filters the way we relate to what comes into the consciousness and also has the energy to purify and release what is already inside of us. The fifth chakra allows for purification of the second chakra and emotional state in two ways—by no longer being swayed in sense of self by other people's perceptions or opinions, and by using authentic and honest communication to heal emotional wounds. By speaking our truth, we express our feelings to the universe and allow these feeling to be released back to the universe. Bottling up thoughts and feelings leads to inner energetic stagnation; communicating openly and honestly is a big key in mental, emotional, and even physical healing.

When a feeling or emotion is not allowed to be expressed, its energy stays confined in the body. Lack of proper communication is one of the biggest problems individuals face in their healing journey. Energy stays stagnant because of an inability to properly communicate what is going on. I strongly encourage everyone, and I mean everyone, to have someone they can talk to. This can be a friend or acquaintance, but a trained counselor or ministerial guide is even better, because they are trained in how to respond in constructive ways. Anything a person can talk about will eventually not have any power over them. Anything a person cannot talk about will eventually destroy them. All mental illness and chronic emotional distress begins with an individual who either cannot effectively communicate what is going on inside or is not heard by the person they are communicating with. Being heard is just as important as communicating truth; a person needs to know their words are heard in order to restore inner balance.

The words we speak are always in some way tied to how we feel. When a person can learn to be clear and direct in communication habits, it is the most powerful and easy tool to use for integrated well-being. The strength and purity cultivated in the second chakra energy will aid in direct and clear communication in life and in return, clear communication will also help to strengthen and cleanse the second chakra of emotional stagnation.

Due to its purifying aspects, this chakra is also the place of consciousness where preconceived notions of purity are reexamined and worked through. Notions of right versus wrong and light versus dark are no longer such well-defined concepts because, after all, our definitions of these things are shaped by thoughts and experiences, not by pure perception. The more work a person does with this chakra consciousness will change their notions of life as a whole into a complex matrix of subtle nuance. By learning to see beyond the surface of things as black or white, it becomes possible to see the depth and the intention behind all things. To see the inner depth of all of life is to purify all of life. The fifth chakra can help with this, and specifically, in understanding what is right and wrong for your individual dharma and overall life path.

People who work a lot with this chakra's energy will often be rule breakers, going against societal norms in pursuit of their own way of doing things. They get to the depth of matters quickly and care more for the real substance and not the façade that is shown to the world. They don't play games with conversation, either. These people often find themselves in leadership or teaching roles due to their clear communication style and direct approach toward life. To work with this chakra's energy is to always have clear, effective, and honest communication with yourself and others. Mantra repetition (any mantra) also further opens up the fifth chakra's energy. *You can also try the "Visualization on Infinite Space" technique in chapter 6.*

Sixth Chakra (Ajna)—
The Command Center

The sixth chakra is known as the Ajna chakra and has only two petals, which represent the coming together of the opposite polarities of life. Because this is a place of unity, it is the place we can command our reality through. At this place of consciousness, everything becomes one. Masculine and feminine are united, light and dark are seen as one, and we can learn to see everything as equally important in life. When no one thing is able to sway a person's consciousness, consciousness can be used to direct the flow of life. Up to this point, other things, circumstances, experiences, people, etc., all have a lot of control over our perceptions and experiences of life. When the consciousness is worked with through the sixth chakra, this trend is reversed and the individual becomes able to project their intentions outward to shape reality.

When the mind is filled with thoughts, visualizing and projecting the intentions you have for your reality is difficult. The clearer the mind becomes, the easier it is to create the reality you can envision because there is less clutter in the way. The sixth chakra is connected to the fourth chakra, which contains the potential for all possibility. When you decide which of these infinite potentials you want to live in life, the sixth chakra is the level of consciousness that is used to project that potential and turn it into reality.

The sixth chakra can also be used to take in information through the "third eye," which is another name for this chakra. Most people think about the sixth chakra as being the psychic center, but this is not entirely accurate. While psychic impulses can definitely come from here, how they are received will always be filtered through the latent impressions and experiences stored in the mind.

A cultural note on this chakra can help give further context to it. In Hindu tradition, women in particular wear a *tilak* on the sixth chakra. It is believed that this red dot keeps away the "evil eye" so that negativity does not enter into one's perceptions. The capacity to project one's reality is also the capacity to be able to protect oneself by keeping negativity away. For example, if a person who lacks ethics or morals works very hard to cultivate this chakra, the projective energy can be used destructively against others. Having psychic abilities does not make a person ethical, which is more reason to cultivate yourself holistically and ensure you understand how to use all of your combined energy to create the reality you want to live. A holistic way to open and work with the sixth chakra is through daily meditative practice and visualization exercises, as are found in chapter 6. *A good meditative technique to start with is the "Technique for Cultivating Intuition & Subtle Awareness" found in chapter 6.*

Manas Chakra— Sensory Impressions

The Manas chakra has already been discussed a bit when talking about the mind. The Manas chakra is what we refer to as the mind, and it governs sensory impression. Because of this connection, the mind can be used as a storehouse of information or can be kept clean so that the sixth chakra can function to its highest capacity. Both the Manas and Indu chakras are connected directly to the sixth chakra and will govern how effectively the sixth chakra works. Learned knowledge is stored throughout the body, thanks to Manas chakra. These stored impressions are the thought forms previously discussed. When left alone, they determine the perceptions of life and dictate how we react to all of life's situations. Through meditation and other forms of spiritual practice and vibrational healing, when thought forms are purged, individuals develop the capacity to clearly respond to a situation instead of react to life based on the impressions stored through the Manas chakra.

To make life conscious, stored conditioning must be eliminated. Consciousness means being in control of decisions at each and every moment, not being reactive to life. Thought forms act to negate willpower, and conversely, cultivating willpower acts to eliminate the stored impressions in the Manas chakra. Meditation and discernment are the easiest ways to work on this level of consciousness, but it takes consistent practice over an extended period of time.

Meditation works to purge stored impressions from the Manas chakra. Any technique relating to water element will also work directly on Manas. Daily contemplation and inner discernment are powerful means for working directly with Manas, as they stimulate the Indu chakra to release the stored impressions in the Manas chakra. Rajas related techniques will also work, as they help bring focus to a particular thing and out of the subconscious burden of the mind. *See the "Technique for Cultivating Mindfulness" in chapter 6 to learn a way to bring your focus where you want it to be.*

Indu Chakra— Intellect and Intelligence

The Indu chakra is located right above the Manas chakra and governs the capacity of intellect. We have also discussed this chakra briefly when discussing the mind. The intellect can be directed either outward as creative capacity or inward as destructive discerning capacity to dissolve the thought forms stored by the Manas chakra. When this energy is directed inward, it is extremely efficient for cultivating sustained well-being because it targets the subtle energy source of problems directly. If the root energy that is causing a physical, mental, or emotional problem is completely destroyed, the problem will not manifest again.

In order to strengthen the sixth chakra, both Manas and Indu need to be understood, because both contribute to how well the sixth chakra functions. There are very important implications. The mind, intellect, and sixth chakra are cumulatively the most powerful things we contain that shape our reality. Energy flows in the manner that these chakras guide it to. Wherever your thoughts are, your energy goes. To effectively heal others or heal yourself, it is important to be in control of your own mind and know how to keep it healthy. Without the directing capacity of these chakras, the potential energy found in any healing modality will not work to its optimal ability. All subtle energy has to be directed, and these combined centers teach us how to do that effectively.

Since the Indu chakra deals with creativity, intellect, and expansion both inwardly and outwardly (as discussed in chapter 2), there are many ways to work with its energy. Contemplation and inner discernment work to take this energy inward. Creative expression such as dance, music, language study, philosophy, and other intellectually stimulating pursuits activate the energy of the Indu chakra.

Seventh Chakra (Sahasrara)— The Crown

The seventh chakra is commonly referred to as the crown chakra. This is the lotus of a thousand petals, which contain the cumulative energy of the six main chakras previously discussed (minus Manas and Indu). The crown chakra relates to our ability to function in a place of unity with both ourselves and the universe at large. It is the place that recognizes we are all made up of the same universal stuff and are all intrinsically connected. For the crown chakra to be opened from within requires all of the other chakra energies being balanced and working in harmony—literally. Since it is composed of the same vibrations of the rest of the chakras, if the vibrations are constricted anywhere in the body, they will also be constricted in the seventh chakra. There is no way to pry this chakra open; it has to happen authentically through integrated mind, body, spirit balance.

When the entire system is in balance, this automatically happens—universal energy flows freely into and through a person. Sometimes this energy is seen as grace, sometimes it is seen as God consciousness, and at other times, just a powerful vibration that could not be obtained from any other place in consciousness. Great saints and visionaries function at this vibratory frequency, working to instill peace, harmony, and cooperative understanding to everyone they meet.

When a person feels alone, this chakra energy is constricted. To be in connection with universal energy, a person will never feel alone or unsupported. Unshakable constant connection to oneself and life as a whole is governed by the crown chakra. There is no way to experience this consciousness without also feeling prosperous, humble, and an overall attitude of giving and supporting the whole creation. Positivity, joy, cooperation, and peace are hallmarks of the energy this chakra emanates.

To work with the seventh chakra's energy, focus your intentions toward making the world a better place. Discover how you can contribute your energy and gifts to help others. This place of unity cannot be experienced solely by focusing on your individual self; work to constantly understand your connection with the world. *You can also use the "Technique for Cultivating Unity" in chapter 6.*

Hridaya Chakra—The Spiritual Heart

The Hridaya chakra is not often discussed, but it is an important place in consciousness to understand. This is the chakra of love, devotion, and ultimate surrender to the will of God. It is considered a mini version of the central point found in the crown chakra, known as bindu, and the same enlightened experiences can happen through this chakra as it is connected directly to the crown chakra. In the Hridaya chakra, all subtle energy channels intersect. It is considered the seat of the entire universe, the soul, God, and everything in existence. It is also known as the chakra of miracles and the ability to exert one's will over the laws of nature and matter. Dharma, dreams, and everything a person is and has the potential to be is found in this chakra's energy.

In ancient cultures, there was no distinction between mind and heart. The mind and heart were recognized as one entity, with thoughts being the surface of the mind and feelings being the depth of one's mind. The Hridaya is the place where thoughts and feelings merge as one. When we can unite these two forces equally, with thoughts always being in alignment with feelings, it is the sure sign of integration, balance, and healthy spiritual growth. Not only does this capacity take a person closer to God and self, it also takes a person closer to fully living their life's purpose. The Hridaya chakra can control the energy of all of the other chakras and regulate the process of life through the currents of love itself.

The Hridaya chakra can only be entered through great love and devotion to the spiritual side of life and to God directly. It is a place of unshakable faith, where all things literally become possible. In this chakra, matter and spirit work in tandem as one. From the standpoint of love, unification, and having all energy within the body work together, this chakra is of utmost importance. Even though the Hridaya chakra is situated below the fourth chakra, it is most closely connected to the crown chakra. In addition to carrying the energy of the crown chakra (which contains the energy of all of the first six chakras as previously discussed), it also is the place where the soul resides and where temperament, guna, and elemental composition arise from. This place of unity between thoughts, feelings, temperament, spirituality, and overall life purpose is what gives rise to what we know as love.

Love is the solution for all constricted or stagnant subtle energy and can instantly unlock all negative feelings and make energy free-flowing. Love heals all wounds, and quickly, when it is allowed to work. It is the most powerful energy of all in vibrational healing. To learn to work with the Hridaya chakra and its energy of unification and love, cultivate a daily spiritual practice. *Some techniques to begin your journey are given in chapter 6, including the "Technique for Cultivating Unity," which works with the energy of the seventh chakra and the Hridaya chakra.*

Three

Understanding Your Energy Type & Temperament (Gunas & Elements)

•••••••••••••

Now that we've established the basics about the chakras and subtle energy, let's take a look at the gunas and elements that directly affect a person's temperament, unique character, and overall physical body composition. Gunas relate primarily to temperament and inner disposition, whereas the elements are what give form and structure to matter and the physical body. Since the gunas and elements are the energies responsible for your unique self and overall life path, learning to work with these energies effectively will be the foundation that enables the energy of each chakra to open and clear out subtle energy blockages. A person's particular combination of gunas and elements will be what makes a particular life path or form of vibrational healing work for an individual. Understanding all of these pieces will give a depth of understanding to how to work with different vibrational healing modalities.

The Gunas (Your Mind and Spirit Energy Type)

The primary building blocks of all nature and matter are the three gunas: sattva, rajas, and tamas. From these three comes a further distillation of the five elements of earth, water, fire, air, and ether, which we will discuss later in this chapter. The gunas (modes of energy) relate strongly to temperament (your basic innate nature as it affects your behavior), character (your unique personality and traits as determined by your decisions), and dharma (your overall life purpose as a reflection of how well you are living your life in accordance with your temperament and character), which is why the gunas need to be understood. It is a person's dharma and soul's dreams that give rise to how the entire mind, body, soul complex works. Dharma manifests through temperament as a specific guna composition and manifests through the physical body as a specific corresponding elemental composition. This is to ensure the structure of the body matches the mind, emotions, and a person's innate life path.

The gunas are, in my opinion, an awesome means of understanding oneself; when you learn to understand them and identify them in life, you can learn to use their strengths and overcome the weaknesses associated with them. There is no such thing as a good guna or bad guna! They all have positive and negative attributes; things that are beneficial to well-being and things that act to constrict well-being. This is the way with most things in life. A sword has two edges: it can be used to protect or cause harm, depending on how it is used. Temperament is the same way. By working with it, individual temperament is a key to living a healthy, fulfilling, successful life. By working against one's temperament, life becomes extremely difficult.

Every person and thing in existence has all three gunas in differing amounts. Which guna governs the psyche will fluctuate throughout the course of a day, week, month, and year. Because they are fundamental parts of temperament, each will seek its expression. This never changes; the only thing that changes is how a person is able to relate to the attributes of each and use them for one's own benefit. Let's look at the attributes of each guna—how they can help, how they can hinder—and learn how to work with them together to accomplish a place of balance and well-being. After learning the attributes, you'll be able to complete a quiz to help you determine your own temperament. The quiz will help you understand the terms we discuss here, which can often seem abstract.

Sattva Guna (Clarity)

Sattva guna can be summed up in one word: clarity. How clear are your perceptions of yourself, of life, of God, of everything that you are and want to become? Sattva guna is an energy that clarifies and brings inner knowledge to life path and purpose. It has the capacity to illuminate, not through itself, but by its capacity to clear away everything that stands in the way of the energy a person already carries. It relates to the concepts of illumination, inner knowledge, peace, harmony, and oneness—all things people aspire for in life. While these external manifestations are not sattva itself, when sattvic energy is used well, it can lead to these very positive life manifestations.

Conversely, when sattvic energy is not used to bring about self-clarity, it is one of the most deceptive and destructive energies in existence. When constricted or misdirected, sattvic energy makes an individual dogmatic, pious, and egocentric in decisions, thought patterns, and actions, with the firmly rooted notion that their way is the best way or only way. Whenever a person disrespects someone else for their beliefs or has the notion of spiritual pride or egoism, it is a negative manifestation of sattvic energy. Light has the capacity to illuminate or to blind. While this energy can definitely bring about humility, true compassion, and love, it can also solidify egoism if its energy is not balanced well with the other gunas.

Working well with sattva comes back to clarity and understanding that each and every person has their own unique life path, struggles, and reason for living. When "our way" is perceived as "the only way" for everyone, clarity is skewed. Tools and techniques can be used by everyone, but when, how, and for what reasons are unique to each and every person. A person who has mastered a true level of inner-clarity will not only know what is best for them, they will also be able to correctly assess which techniques will work best for another person.

Sattva guna also brings about peace, which can be both good and bad. If there is an insistence on always being peaceful, then nothing will ever get done. Being at peace negates the desire or motivation for change. Change and dynamic movement are an intrinsic part of life, so to try and always hold onto an external manifestation of peace is to negate the process of life and how the universe functions. When sattva is manifested positively, it gives people the understanding of unlimited possibility. There are no bounds on the potential of life, other than what a person won't work for or cannot perceive. Sattva is the clear perception piece of the puzzle of life.

The gunas will also affect a person's taste in foods and lifestyle activities. Sattvic energy makes people want nutritious, easily digestible foods, a peaceful overall lifestyle, and time for solitude. It's responsible for deep introspection, which is required to have true clarity and an overall feeling of contentment in life. *Many of the techniques in chapter 6 work with sattva guna, including the "Technique for Cultivating Unity" and "Technique for New Growth and Positive Change."*

Rajas Guna (Confidence and Focused Energy)

Rajas is the energy responsible for desire, movement, and focused activity. We've learned about desire already in connection with the third chakra. If desire is moving in a direction to bring about life purpose and fulfillment, it is a great thing. If it is being used to further selfish desires that don't take a person to their full potential, they are extremely negative. The root of rajas is *raj*, which in Sanskrit means "royal." A kingly or queenly presence and energy comes from rajas and its ability to constantly move and be active. Since the universe as a whole is always moving and changing, being in tune with this helps individuals to be in the flow of their own dynamic energy and the universal energies too.

Two words that greatly summarize rajas guna are confidence and ambition. It takes a very dynamic, empowered energy to lead, create, and really get things done in life. Rajas is the underlying vital energy that motivates people to act. Nothing in the world would be sustained without action; because of that, this ability to be dynamic is also linked to maintenance and preservation. We eat, exercise, work, live, and enjoy life as a way of maintaining life. Actions and desires further the purpose for living. With no desire and no ambition, life would be stagnant and unfulfilling. Rajas gives the needed energy to pursue one's dreams and desires, and sustain life as a whole.

Some negative manifestations of rajas are anger, hyperactivity, and unending, unfocused desires. It comes down to how this energy is directed and utilized. If there is clarity of what needs to be done in life, rajas can act very powerfully and dynamically to take a person toward that goal. If there is not clarity of purpose on what actions are beneficial, rajas energy can lead to frustration and agitation because of the inability to focus on a solid goal. Because rajas energy is very dynamic, it always needs to be directed toward a positive goal through strong intention and focused willpower. It does not wait around for something to follow. Rajas leads the way, just like royalty should. It'll happily take competent direction, but won't wait around for guidance to show up. A person looking to cultivate strong leadership skills would benefit from cultivating their dynamic, rajas energy.

In the mind, rajas can manifest as numerous desires, numerous projects to accomplish, and an overall liking of vibrancy and activity. When rajas is dominant in the physical body, people like to remain active and are rarely overweight. It gives the needed energy to work hard, long hours and to constantly be on the go. Rajas gives a craving for flavorful and spicy foods, even if they are not easily digestible. Emotionally, rajas can cause problems when desires are not met (usually due to the inability to focus on a single desire), because obstructed desires lead to frustration and anger.

There are techniques in chapter 6 that work with rajasic energy including the "Meditation Technique for Cultivating Healing Energy" and "Technique for Cultivating Inner Prosperity."

Tamas Guna (Solid Foundations)

Tamas is responsible for solidity, gravity, sleep, and solid foundations. It's the energy that holds the physical body together as a human body, not a body of light or sound. Tamas is probably the most misunderstood guna because people who don't live a balanced life are not capable of using its energy productively. Since the nature of its energy is to constrict and contain, it requires a disciplined being to work well with it. Tamas relates to the unconscious energy we all carry; it's the energy responsible for keeping the physical body together, taking care of innate biological responses in the body, sleep, regeneration, and all of the combined energies we never think about that keep the physical body working well.

What tamas guna provides is crucial for life. Sleep is an important thing; it's regenerative and brings about healing. Solid foundations are very important to successful living. The key to working with this energy is discipline and consistency. If a person sleeps too much, they will become dull and lethargic. If you don't take care of yourself properly, you'll suffer the consequences in life. The thing to remember is that foundations are just that: foundations. They are only a starting point to build upon, not to indulge in. With proper downtime, rest, relaxation, healthy intake of food, good hygiene, and so forth, there is nothing that cannot be accomplished. This is all Life 101; it's a system of personal conduct and values that require responsibility and commitment to life. Negative attributes that come from tamasic energy include sloth, inertia, laziness, lack of ability to change, excessive sleep, and poor hygiene. People who don't want to or seem incapable of making change in life are trapped by the energy of tamas guna.

When there is excess tamasic energy in the physical body, people will be overweight and in poor health. Tamas in the mind shows up as rigidity, dullness, and in extreme cases, lack of ability to understand basic concepts such as right and wrong. When in excess, it negates the ability of proper discernment. On an emotional level, excessive tamas causes sadness and discord. It keeps people stuck in the same lifestyle pattern repeatedly with a seeming inability to adapt to new ways of doing things. Food-wise, it creates a craving for excessive sugar, sweets, leftover foods that have lost much of their vitality, foods that are extremely dense and difficult to digest, and an overall indulgence in food.

Tamas is the easiest energy to dispel because it only takes getting up and doing something to move into a rajasic state. Sattvic energy is the most difficult to change because it is so subtle and can be deceptive. Despite this, more people are trapped by the negative attributes of tamas than they are sattva. Societally we are taught to look for easy or quick solutions to problems, which contributes to an overall lack of discipline. Lack of disciplined living increases the amount of tamasic energy a person carries. The easiest way to counteract the negative attributes of tamasic energy is to exercise the physical body. *You can also work with the "Technique for Cultivating Inner Prosperity" in chapter 6.*

When there is an emphasis placed on balance in life, all three gunas will be understood as equally important. No one guna should take priority over any other; they all need to be understood for what they are, how they are beneficial and how they make up each person's unique temperament and constitution.

Temperament & Life-Path Tendencies

Sattva: People with sattvic dispositions will gravitate more toward pursuits which contribute to conceptual clarity, intellectual understanding and an overall "big-picture" way of perceiving life. They tend to be the people who have a visionary or idealistic approach to life. Oftentimes healers fall into this category, because restoring health is restoring peace to the body, and sattva is about peace, harmony, and sustenance. Teachers, peacemakers, professors, ministers, life coaches, etc., fall into this category of temperament. People with a sattvic disposition will give off an energy of lightness, expansiveness, and depth to their character which can't quite be described through tangible feeling; it's the perception created due to a prominence of air and ether elements. Sattvic people who really know how to work their energy well are dreamy and otherworldly, but not all know how to put their best foot forward. When these people haven't balanced their energy effectively, they can come across as zealots for their chosen beliefs and cause great harm to many people. The outspoken haters in society, religious fanatics, and the most negative people imaginable have not learned how to use their sattvic disposition effectively. Being illumined, or more appropriately thinking you are illumined when really you have not integrated your expansiveness, can lead to a mighty ego problem.

Rajas: While the sattvic idealists want to be the changemakers because of their visionary capacity, it takes a person with a strong rajasic disposition, and the intense focus and fire that goes with that to actually go out and be the one making change. A person with a rajasic disposition will know what they want and be willing to work for it. Since rajas relates to charisma, poise, and character, these people are the leaders in society. Rajasic people tend to lead from the front, whereas sattvic people may advise a rajasic counterpart or lead from behind a charismatic leader. Activists and people who really want to make a difference in the world will have a strong rajasic disposition to their temperament. So do successful business owners, entrepreneurs, media personalities, dancers, politicians, rock stars, and the like. Even doctors, firefighters, and emergency medical professionals fall into this category because of their ability to work adeptly under pressure. Fire and rajas create pressure on the mind and body, so those who thrive well in these environments will be apt to have a strong rajasic disposition. Society's true knights in shining armor fall into this category of people. Another trait you will find with people with a rajasic inclination is their ability to draw attention, for better or worse. This can be through motivation and inspiration of others or through a brash, arrogant self-centeredness. Regardless of how these people get attention, they usually end up in the limelight due to their charisma, uncanny charm, and determination to succeed.

Tamas: People with more earthy and tamasic inclinations will be the best ones to put in charge of management, as they tend to be very detail oriented and have strong multitasking and organizational skills. These people know how to strategically manage an initiative once it's been created and build solid foundations for things to ground from. Writers, editors, managers, organization leaders, and great communicators often fall into this category of people. Because of the need to build solid foundations in life, these people are inclined toward liking stability and have a no-nonsense approach toward life; wasting time is not their forte because to build a solid foundation, you have to work diligently and consistently toward a goal. These people can also serve as great counselors and guides because of their grounded nature. If people who are very earthy and tamasic have too much of that grounding energy that causes inertia, these people are the most difficult to get moving in a good life direction. These are the people who would be apt to waste their lives in confusion and sloth because of the overabundance of inertia in the body, mind, and emotions.

Guna & Temperament Quiz

Here's the part you've been waiting for. Use the quiz here to determine a base point for your temperament! You'll also be able to do a similar quiz for your elemental composition. By better understanding your temperament and body composition, you can determine what sort of temperament and elemental healing modalities would be best to explore for your personal healing journey (discussed in chapters 4 and 5).

For each of the series of questions below, put a number 1 in the box that best answers the question, leaving the remaining two boxes blank. Once all questions in each series are answered, add up the totals in each column, then multiply the total points by 4, 2, or 0 as specified in the box under the corresponding points. Add all three scores together to get your total score in each category.

Here is an example so you can directly see how to do the scoring:

Questions for Sattva:	Mostly Yes	Some-times	Mostly No
1. I enjoy deep contemplation.		1	
2. I enjoy spending some time by myself every day.			1
3. Spicy foods are aggravating to my body.		1	
4. I enjoy deep philosophical or spiritual inquiry.	1		
5. I enjoy studying something to truly learn its essence.		1	
6. I truly want to make the world a better place.	1		
7. I seek to understand my place in the world and to understand myself.	1		
8. I want to understand how the universe functions on a fundamental level.			1
9. I want to learn about the spiritual side of life and my spiritual self.	1		
10. I need to understand concepts and mechanisms clearly for me to understand reality. Without understanding "how" things work, I cannot relate well to a concept.		1	
11. I have a sense of optimism and perceive the beauty in life.		1	
Total Points:	4	5	2
Now multiply the points above by the number in each box, then get the score:	Points x 4 = 16	Points x 2 = 10	Points x 0 = 0
Add the scores in all three boxes above for a total Sattva Score:	26		

 Answer each question by how your actions really are, not what you want them to be or aspire toward. Be honest with yourself so you can accurately assess the types of modalities that will best benefit you right now. The guna and temperament quiz is meant to help you understand your inner being and psychological disposition. Once you have your results, look back to the gunas to learn more about your dominant one and how it affects your perceptions of life.

Questions for Sattva:	Mostly Yes	Some-times	Mostly No
1. I enjoy deep contemplation.	|		
2. I enjoy spending some time by myself every day.	|		
3. Spicy foods are aggravating to my body.		/	
4. I enjoy deep philosophical or spiritual inquiry.	/		
5. I enjoy studying something to truly learn its essence.		|	
6. I truly want to make the world a better place.	|		
7. I seek to understand my place in the world and to understand myself.	|		
8. I want to understand how the universe functions on a fundamental level.		|	
9. I want to learn about the spiritual side of life and my spiritual self.	|		

10. I need to understand concepts and mechanisms clearly for me to understand reality. Without understanding "how" things work, I cannot relate well to a concept.		/	
11. I have a sense of optimism and perceive the beauty in life.	/		
Total Points:	7	4	
Now multiply the points above by the number in each box, then get the score:	Points x 4 = 28	Points x 2 = 8	Points x 0 =
Add the scores in all three boxes above for a total Sattva Score:	36		

Questions for Rajas:	**Mostly Yes**	**Some-times**	**Mostly No**
1. I have a very active social life and I enjoy it.		|	
2. I am very focused on a specific thought or project.		|	
3. I like to stay busy and active.	4	|	
4. I like working on puzzles that keep my mind engaged.		|	
5. I enjoy the taste of spicy foods.		|	
6. I work hard to accomplish my dreams.		|	
7. I change quickly. I embrace change even when it's difficult.	|		
8. I enjoy leading and giving direction to others and I'm good at it.		|	
9. I like being a focal point of attention or often find myself as one.	.	|	

10. I have a strong sense of duty and obligation to life.		*1*	
11. I work hard and push through all obstacles and resistance.		*1*	
Total Points:		*10*	
Now multiply the points above by the number in each box, then get the score:	Points x 4 = *4*	Points x 2 = *20*	Points x 0 =
Add the scores in all three boxes above for a total Rajas Score:	*24*		

Questions for Tamas:	Mostly Yes	Some-times	Mostly No
1. I don't want to contemplate. Just tell me the answers.			*1*
2. I don't enjoy physical activity. I prefer to sit and watch.		*1*	
3. I am considered moderately to extremely overweight.	*1*		
4. I prefer salty and sugary foods to fresh fruits and vegetables.	*4 1*		
5. I have very rigid ideals about reality and I don't want to change.			*1*
6. The important parts of life comes down to food, sex, and personal gratification.		*1*	
7. I don't deal well with problems. I avoid or run away from them.			*1*
8. I have no idea what I want to do with my life or feel very confused.			*1*
9. I am prone to depression.			*1*
10. I suffer from many health problems or a single severe problem.			*1*

11. I tend to focus on the past.		\	
Total Points:	2	3	6
Now multiply the points above by the number in each box, then get the score:	Points x 4 = 8	Points x 2 = 6	Points x 0 =
Add the scores in all three boxes above for a total Tamas Score:	14		

Now take the total score from all three above and write it here:

Sattva Score: ___36___

Rajas Score: ___24___

Tamas Score: ___14___

The scores from the quiz above (and the elemental quiz you will take soon) are meant to be a guidepost for you to understand your relative composition in terms of gunas and elements. It's not meant to label you as "sattvic," "rajasic," or "tamasic," because that would not be accurate. We all have differing proportions of all the gunas and all the elements inside. Having a higher score in a particular area or two will give you a good place to start when exploring healing modalities (and combination modalities that mix gunas and elements) in chapter six.

The Five Elements
(Your Physical Energy Type)

Further distinctions from the three gunas are the five elements. All of matter, including the physical and subtle body, contains the energy of the elements. While gunas relate more to temperament and inner disposition, elements relate more to the physical manifestations of a particular combination of gunas. The five elements—earth, water, fire, air, and ether—are situated in the center of the first five chakras, respectively, with earth element in the root chakra and so on (the chakras are laid out for your reference in a chart on page 55). The elements range from the most subtle element of ether (also known as space) all the way down to the densest manifestation of earth element, from which all matter is created. There is tangible earth all the way to the void of space and everything in between.

Since elements are physical manifestations of temperament, they can be used as powerful, tangible tools in health and healing. Each element has its corresponding sensory capacity of smell, taste, sight, touch, and sound, respectively. When you can identify what is out of balance, why, and all of the pieces that need to be worked with, choosing the modalities are easy. It's the understanding of what is needed and why that takes incredible discernment and perception. Let's look at the fundamental nature of each of the elements.

Earth Element

Earth element is situated in the first chakra. Earth element is like the ground itself; dense, rigid, and mostly non-moving. It's solid, gives a base of support, and provides nourishment for things to grow. Earth element contains the subtle essence of all of the other elements inside of it, making it a little bit of everything. Earth element is intrinsically connected with the sense of smell—a very primal sensation that we can use to sense whether things are on track or not. You can smell a good or bad situation, so to speak! You can also smell a good partner because of pheromones. While that is not something we consciously understand, it is an underlying factor in how we relate to people and life situations on a primal level.

Earth element provides rigid structure to the body and to life. It's the container that everything else flows through. When people have a lot of earth element in their physical constitution, they will be robust individuals, although quite possibly short and dense in stature. Because it is earth that carries all nutrients in it, it's raw and powerful. People with a lot of earth element will also come across as having a lot of power, even if it is only in potential. In terms of temperament and character, earth element lends to a rigid, fixed thought process that has solid goals, ideas, and no ambiguity. This can be good or bad, depending on whether these ideas are constructive or not. *See chapter 6 for specific earth element techniques to practice, including a "Gemstone-Charged Water Technique."*

Water Element

Water element is located in the second chakra. Water element contains the vibrations of all the elements except for earth element in its subtle composition. Water element is extremely adaptable as it represents the ability to flow. It carries nutrients and hydration to all parts of the body and is related to the sense of taste. Temperament-wise, water represents the ability to change ideas, to move, to grow and to go with the flow of life. Water constitutes nearly 70 percent of the physical body, making it more abundant than earth element in the body and one of the most powerful elements to understand in healing and maintaining physical, mental, and emotional health.

Water takes on the shape of whatever container it is put in. Water can also be found as a solid, liquid, or gas, showing how it takes on the energy of what is affecting it. Water, over time, can even erode rocks and great mountains. It's a deceptively powerful element that is oftentimes underestimated. Since water element is found in the second chakra, it is also connected with feelings and emotions, which are extremely fluid and always changing. Just like water, feelings take on the structure and energy of what has created them. Water can be used to wash away anything that is unwanted including negative feelings; its greatest gift is in its always-moving nature.

Water element will take on the vibrations of whatever is around or in it. It can be used to absorb positive vibrations of just about anything, which can work to charge an environment with whatever energy a person is looking to cultivate. People who have a lot of water element in their constitution would be wise to keep good company, because they have the natural inclination to be like whomever they are around. If company is positive and successful, watery people will naturally conform to this energy of success. If people are negative or bad influences, watery people are apt to also become this way. *See chapter 6 for "Water Element Cleansing Technique," "Mantra-Charged Water Technique," and more techniques to work with water element.*

Fire Element

Fire element is located in the third chakra. It contains the subtle essence of fire, air, and ether elements, but not water or earth elements. Fire is responsible for digestion and is tied to both creation and destruction, but primarily destruction. Fire element, which is connected to the sense of sight, brings the capacities of willpower, focus, and determination. It does this by destroying everything else that is not a person's focal point. Destruction is a vital process for well-being, eliminating what is no longer useful to life.

Fire is the capacity of transformation, both physically and subtly. Physically, food is digested and transformed into energy and nutrients. Fire destroys the container energy is in, so as to unleash the energy itself and redirect it for other purposes. For example, a disease manifestation such as a tumor needs to be destroyed. The energy inside the tumor has to be redirected toward healthy bodily functions, which is only possible once the tumor is gone. Energy itself is neutral; it needs intentionality behind it to function in a particular way. When one container is destroyed, energy can either go toward other purposes or be used to create a new container.

Subtly, fire is used to destroy thoughts and desires, which would eventually form the basis of a solid physical manifestation. If a person has ten desires, fire element can be used to dissolve nine of them, directing the power behind those nine desires toward the manifestation of the one remaining one. When something is held in single pointed focus, it is cultivated energetically. The more that a single thing is focused upon, fire acts to destroy everything else.

Learning to work with fire energy is important for learning how to manifest the things you want and need in life and in learning to let go of things you really don't need. Love is like fire and its subtle essence is contained within a fire region found in the spiritual heart center. Love is also single pointed and intensely focused, although love is so broad it can contain much more than a limited desire. Desire itself is a type of fire. The creation and destruction energies associated with fire are two sides of the same coin; where you have one, you will have the other. Fire also holds the energy of preservation, but only when it has consumed everything but itself. Contemplate the intensity and power of fire in relation to desires and you can gain a lot of insight into how thoughts and desires shape a person's life path.

See chapter 6 for several fire element techniques including "Visualization for Cultivating Subtle Energy" and Pranayama Technique for Dissipating Negative Energy."

Air Element

Air element is located in the fourth chakra. Air element contains only the subtle essence of air and ether elements, and as such, has very little density. It is related to the sense of touch. Air element is important to life because of the prana it carries and its intrinsic lightness. Air element is also tied to thought and how thought travels through the body. If it were not for air, thoughts would not be able to move or form at all. Aggravations in air element can cause disturbance in the mind including excessive thoughts and worrying.

Most everyone has heard the term "airhead" before, summarizing what happens when people get disconnected from reality. Because air element gives rise to lightness and uplifting energies, it also has the capacity to sweep people off of the ground, so to speak, in how a person relates to all aspect of life. Air element is very important for personal expansion and growth, but has to be balanced well with earth, water, and fire elements to live a productive, engaging life. When not in balance, people develop a tendency of living in their thoughts alone; a self-created dream world, which acts as a barrier to integrated living. Having new ideas and the capacity to be expansive is wonderful, but to bring any of it to fruition requires grounding and commitment to an idea. The nature of air is that it is always moving and free-flowing. Too much of this energy leads to a lack of commitment and follow-through and the inability to complete projects before jumping to a new idea.

Both air and ether elements are powerful forces to help an individual connect to higher and more expansive realms of consciousness. To work positively with air element, it can be used as an uplifting force that counteracts the gravity and density of the mind, or any limiting thought or belief pattern. Air is cleansing and holds lots of pranic energy; this increased prana combined with the movement of air in the body has the capacity to "blow away" stagnant energies and replace their presence with life-giving prana. The art of pranayama revolves around breathing exercises that increase prana or move prana in different parts of the body to target energy blockages and mental or emotional issues.

The more expansive an individual is and the more prana taken in through breathing, the less food will need to be consumed. Hunger is an interesting thing and definitely not something understood well by modern Western science or medicine. When there is lots of prana, hunger ceases. When there is an absence of prana, hunger increases. This is something to contemplate deeply on if you want to really understand how prana and subtle energy in general work in the body.

Without air, people would not have the capacity to perceive reality through the sense of touch. A person who has sensitivity to or extreme liking of touch will work well with air element. Touch is a way of connecting with something outside of oneself and air is a mode of energy that moves things. Sometimes new experiences and perceptions are needed in life. Learning to work with air element effectively can help a person breathe new life into every experience and alter the way in which reality is perceived by lightening the density of experience. Too much rigidity in life is not healthy. Air element and its expansive nature can help to bring balance and a fresh perspective into the seemingly mundane aspects of life, which are in fact, never as mundane as they may seem. *See "Pranayama Technique for Building Subtle Energy" and more techniques for air element in chapter 6.*

Ether Element

Ether element is located in Vishuddha, the fifth chakra, and is connected to the sense of sound. Ether element contains only the subtle element of ether in it, which is also known as space. Space is not always thought of as an element, but it definitely is one! Even modern physics has recently been able to show this through studies of gravity in relation to planets and how they inhabit space. Space can bend and stretch itself; as such, it is the fabric everything else is created in.

The Vedas teach that the entire universe has been created from the sound current. Physics is catching up to this with its concept of string theory. Sound is an aspect of vibrational frequency that gives rise to all of creation. Even light, according to the Vedas, comes from the sound current. Sounds have both audible and inaudible frequencies associated with their energy as well as light or color.

Because sound is the basis of all different vibrations, mantra is an extremely diverse tool to use in healing to correct imbalances and eliminate stuck or stagnant energy in the body. Mantra gets right to the root of the subtle body and subtle energy to make a change from the inside out. There are mantras for just about anything, but to use them effectively they should come under the guidance of a qualified guru or teacher. Because of the energy they carry, some can be harmful if that person is not adequately prepared to work with their energy. Just like the example of a 60-watt lightbulb trying to handle 200 watts of current. It's not going to work very well.

Sound for healing does not have to come from mantra; it can come from music, voice, instruments, drums, animal calls, running water, nature sounds, or anything that produces a vibratory current. Since sound is usually connected to other elements in addition to ether, it is an excellent modality to delve into and contemplate for complex issues. For example, the sounds of a river are connected to both ether and water elements and the second chakra. Remember, the second chakra is a vast place of how people perceive themselves and water controls our ability to go with the flow, to heal and to change. Water sounds from a river or ocean can be used for many different reasons and to heal different aspects of the psyche, emotions, and body. Contemplating this and other similar examples will help in understanding the myriad of ways a combination of elemental modalities can be used for health and healing.

Even sounds as seemingly simple as words have powerful vibrations to them. All words carry energy with them that can be felt and understood even on a conscious level, so think about what words are doing on a subconscious level. Words themselves have the power to heal or harm; affirmation and mantra create positivity and inner prosperity while harmful words break down a person's inner prosperity and self-worth.

Mantra, sound, and space-based techniques all work on ether element. See "Visualization on Infinite Space" technique and "Mantra-Charged Water Technique" in chapter 6 as good techniques to start with.

I personally connect with sound greater than any of the other elements. I love music, mantra, speaking, singing, and hearing the cacophony of the world at large. Sound is the conduit for me to best allow all other modes of expression to enter through. Which element elicits the greatest response in you? Let's find out!

Elemental Composition Quiz

The elemental composition quiz is designed to help you understand your physical body type. Use the same scoring system as in the temperament quiz. Just as with the temperament quiz, answer each question *by how your actions really are*, not what you want them to be or aspire toward. What you want to be and what you are may not be the same thing. Be honest with yourself so that you can understand yourself.

Questions for Ether Element:	Mostly Yes	Some-times	Mostly No
1. I love music. Music deeply inspires me!	I		
2. For a spiritual practice, I enjoy chanting or listening to mantras.		I	
3. Sounds can either easily relax or agitate me.	I		
4. I like staring at the sky, either at night or during the day.		I	
5. The concept of outer space is interesting to me.		I	
6. I can feel vibration in my body at times.		I	
7. Music or sound can make me think an entirely different way.	*2*	*2* I	
8. I enjoy the concept of nothingness.	I		
9. I enjoy contemplating about the nature of time and how it works.		I	
10. Clear communication is important to me.	I		
Total Points:	*4*	*6*	
Now multiply the points above by the number in each box, then get the score:	Points x 4 = *16*	Points x 2 = *12*	Points x 0 =
Add the scores in all three boxes above for a total Ether Element Score:		*28* 28	

Questions for Air Element:	Mostly Yes	Some-times	Mostly No
1. I am either tall or tend toward being thin and willowy in body type.			I

2. I tend to have a lot of thoughts or am inclined toward worry.			\
3. I enjoy the sensation of touch.	\		
4. Massage makes me feel relaxed.		\	
5. I like to be expansive and open in my perceptions of life.	I		
6. I have difficulty focusing on a project or task at hand.		I	
7. I am an ideas person, and like forming an idea more than working toward it.		I	
8. I am not fond of heavy foods and prefer light, healthy choices.			I
9. My skin tends to be dry.		\	
10. My physical stamina and endurance are low.		I	
Total Points:	2	5	3
Now multiply the points above by the number in each box, then get the score:	Points x 4 = 8	Points x 2 = 10	Points x 0 =
Add the scores in all three boxes above for a total Air Element Score:	18		

Questions for Fire Element:	Mostly Yes	Some- times	Mostly No
1. I am a very focused individual and enjoy things that require my intense focus.		I	
2. I have a healthy appetite and tend to need a lot of food.		\	
3. I am very ambitious.		I	
4. My hair is thin or prematurely gray.			I

	Mostly Yes	Sometimes	Mostly No
5. I prefer cool climates and don't like to be overly hot and/or enjoy cooling foods and drink.			I
6. I have a tendency to get angry or irritated quickly.			I
7. I can gain or lose weight quickly when I work for it.		I	
8. I have a medium build to my body.			I
9. I want what I want when I want it and generally lack patience.			I
10. While I don't need a fire to stay warm, I love being around fire.		I	
Total Points:		5	5
Now multiply the points above by the number in each box, then get the score:	Points x 4 =	Points x 2 = 10	Point x 0 =
Add the scores in all three boxes above for a total Fire Element Score:		10	

Questions for Water Element:	Mostly Yes	Some-times	Mostly No
1. I am very emotional or sentimental in nature.	I		
2. I am empathic or easily tune into and feel other people's feelings.	I		
3. I love being in or near water.	I		
4. My moods change frequently.	I		
5. I can get sad or emotionally down quickly.	+	9	
6. I tend to follow the guidance of someone I trust.	I	9	
7. I love the moon!	I		

8. I can easily listen to others and understand their point of view.		1	
9. I love the tastes and experience of good food and drink!	1		
10. I have a difficult time establishing personal boundaries.	1		
Total Points:	7	3	
Now multiply the points above by the number in each box, then get the score:	Points x 4 = 28	Points x 2 = 6	Points x 0 =
Add the scores in all three boxes above for a total Water Element Score:	34		

Questions for Earth Element:	**Mostly Yes**	**Some-times**	**Mostly No**
1. I have pretty fixed ideas about life, but tend to see the big picture.		1	
2. I have a strong love for home, family, or traditions.		1	
3. I have strong organizational abilities.		1	
4. I am slow to get moving and/ or I tend to gain weight easily.	1	4	
5. I enjoy being in nature, amongst the trees and earth.	1		
6. Fragrances strongly affect me. I love the smell of something nice!		1	
7. I enjoy consistency in life and tend to plan my activities in advance.		1	
8. I love heavy foods like pasta and potatoes, and it takes me a while to digest my food.			1

9. I have a curvy physique or curly hair.	(		
10. My skin tends to be oily.			(
Total Points:	3	5	
Now multiply the points above by the number in each box, then get the score:	Points x 4 = 12	Points x 2 = 10	Points x 0 =
Add the scores in all three boxes above for a total Earth Element Score:	2 2		

Ether Element Score: ___28___

Air Element Score: ___18___

Fire Element Score: ___10___

Water Element Score: ___34___

Earth Element Score: ___22___

Sattva
water.

The Mixture of Gunas & Elements

Gunas and elements are different but strongly interrelated. Where the elements are tangible manifestations we can see and experience, gunas relate to attributes and temperament. The more easily they can be understood in conjunction with one another, the easier it will be to understand all of the other interrelated pieces of mind, body, soul balance.

As you can see in the chart below, earth and water elements are considered part of tamas guna. Air and ether element are considered a part of sattva guna due to their attributes. Fire element is considered part of rajas guna. While rajas can overlap and at times contain both air and water, this is rare in how those elements typically manifest themselves in a person's temperament, but never rule anything out.

Element	Guna	Chakra	Positive Attributes	Negative Attributes
Earth	Tamas— foundation	1st Muladhara	Management, writing, organization, strategy, building solid foundations, consistency, healthy sleep	Laziness, sloth, inertia, excessive sleep, poor diet, lack of exercise, no discipline, lack of life path clarity
Water	Tamas— foundation Rajas— focused intention (sometimes)	2nd Svadhisthana	Flowing, healing, solid sense of self, healthy boundaries, adaptive, self-esteem, changeable	Lack of self-confidence, negative attitude, gloomy, controlled by emotions, no sense of self, lack of distinctive personality (always changes)
Fire	Rajas— focused intentions	3rd Manipura	Focus, will power, confidence, desires, can-do attitude, proactive, dynamic, leadership, determination, authority, regal presence	Anger, excessive desires, scattered thoughts, lack of focus, no follow through on ideas, domineering, power hungry, aggressive, abusive

| Air | Sattva—clarity Rajas—focused intention (sometimes) 15% | 4th Anahata | Subtle awareness, intuition, open to possibility, expanded 3 | Detachment from life, not grounded, flakey, non-committal, lack of focus and follow though |
| Ether | Sattva—clarity | 5th Vishuddha | Neutral to praise or blame, 2 awareness, clear communication, honesty 30% | Disregard for rules, disrespectful of authority, dishonest |

Further Determining
Your Composition & Temperament

Let's look at ways to help you identify both the composition of your temperament and the composition of your elemental makeup. While you've already taken a quiz to get an idea of both, we're going to dive even deeper here through intuitive practice. There are two main ways to determine a person's elemental composition. The first way is based on self-inquiry. Take a piece of paper and write each of the five elements down. Now that you have an idea of what the different elements represent, pick which element is most appealing to you. Write down the number one next to the element you feel most drawn toward. Go through the remaining four elements and rank them from two to five, with two being the next element that appeals to you most, and so on. Depending on how well you know yourself, this exercise might take some time to complete. If it comes easily, excellent! If not, keep working at it and don't worry. This is just a starting point to learning more about yourself.

Once you've identified the two elements you feel most drawn toward, you can take a look at some of the elemental modalities that correspond to your favorite elements in the next chapter. Do they look appealing to you? Does it feel like a fit? If so, you've correctly identified your composition based on your preferences and inclinations. Take a look at your least favorite element and the modalities that correspond with it. Do they seem unappealing? Do you feel mysteriously drawn to them even though you don't really like them? All of this is important to consider. Oftentimes the element we feel least drawn to is the one within the body and mind that needs the most healing. It's not necessarily the weakest element, but could be the most out of balance. Through time with continued contemplation and inner discernment, it is possible to tease out the differences between what you really are in your core makeup versus what you perceive yourself to be outwardly. It's okay if your initial assessment does not turn out to be fully accurate; it's a gauge of where you are now and what all needs to be brought into balance.

The second way to learn about your elemental composition is by having an astrological chart done because each planet corresponds with an element. A good astrologer will be able to determine your elemental makeup based on your chart. I don't recommend this way because it's a quick fix that does not really teach anyone about their own self. If someone else tells you what you are, this negates the process of self-discovery, which is essential for maintaining life balance and excellent physical, mental, and emotional health. Not being in touch with your own self is how negative experiences and illnesses seem to come out of the blue. There are always clues and warning signs; it's merely a question of perception and if an individual is perceptive enough to read the signs they are given. Subtle perception is required for a person to work effectively with subtle energy. Start the process of cultivating subtle perception by analyzing your own nature and character. Once you have an idea of your elemental composition, if you want to check your work with an astrologer, go for it. Both combined can be used as a learning tool, but do try and do the work yourself accurately first.

After you have ranked each of the elements, try to determine what percentage of each you feel inside (you might get an idea from the quiz you took earlier as well). This will further assist you when deciding what techniques in chapter 6 to learn first. Elements are not equally divided in their ratios within an individual. Two people could have the same one through five ranking and end up with a different overall guna composition. After the elemental composition and percentages are determined, look at which gunas these relate to. Earth and water elements relate to

tamas guna, fire relates to rajas guna, and air and ether relate to sattva guna. Sometimes, water and air can also relate
to rajas, but this is more from a temperament perspective
than a physical body composition perspective. Let's look at
this example below:

Element	Guna	1-5 Ranking	Percentage
Earth	Tamas—foundation	2	25%
Water	Tamas—foundation Rajas—focused intention	4	15%
Fire	Rajas—focused intention	3	25%
Air	Sattva—clarity Rajas—focused intention	5	5%
Ether	Sattva—clarity	1	30%

This person is apt to be pretty down-to-earth in nature but also have a lot of conceptual clarity that would
draw them to spiritual or philosophical pursuits. A person who seems near equally split between tamasic and
sattvic traits could approach healing effectively according to either healing modality approach: elemental or
guna correspondences. That said, the temperament (guna)
based approach would probably work better as a starting point because it would give gratification to both the
mind and body. For someone with a predominance of
earth or water though, don't ever neglect the body and
the capacity of sensory stimulation in healing. Tangible

earthy things, fragrances, and spices would all work well for a person with this composition.

The exercise above will serve as a baseline approach in self-discovery. Looking at elemental composition can definitely help in understanding a person's temperament. Since temperament can manifest in so many different ways, understanding the basics of it will help in understanding the types of activities that are apt to bring the most success and fulfillment in life. The difficulty in working with temperament comes into play when temperament and body composition are not being lived in alignment with each other. If one is out of balance, the other will be too because they are different sides of the same coin. The body is merely an extension of temperament and is designed so a person can best live their temperament, so the two have to work as one. Lack of harmony between the temperament and body composition contributes to faulty perceptions of who a person is and what a person needs to do to be successful in life.

If there is a predominance of fire, air, or ether in a person's elemental composition, strongly consider the temperament approach to healing. Things of a fiery, airy, or spacey nature lend themselves toward a strong inclination to really understand the workings of the world and oneself. For someone of this nature, understanding how the process works and why it is being done will be equally as important as undergoing the process itself. Conceptual clarity is important for an intellectually expansive, creative person to really connect with any activity being pursued.

Now that we've discussed these building blocks of both subtle and physical constitution, let's take a look at the physical body itself before we finally dive into discovering the healing modalities that are your best match.

Temperament, Elements & the Physical Body

The physical body is the densest form of subtle energy there is. It's a manifestation of all of the combined energies a person carries inside. In fact, the body itself can be thought of as just a denser form of energy of everything that is more subtle in nature. Not only is temperament seen through the physical body, temperament is what determines the structure of the physical body. Whether a person is tall, short, hefty, willowy, strong, weak, voluptuous, or petite is all determined by temperament—both innate temperament and how well the innate temperament is being lived through life. It's the temperament that determines a person's elemental composition, and it's the elemental composition that plays a major role in the shape and style of the body.

When bringing the body into a place of balance and overall well-being, it is possible to change the way the physical body looks through a process of strengthening attributes in one's temperament. The body type itself will not change, but the way in which the body carries itself can. For example, holding excess weight in the abdominal region can show a softness and lack of willpower or focus in the psyche of a person. Remember, fire element is situated in the third chakra at the navel point. When fire element is robust and strong, digestion will also be robust and strong. Willpower will be strong. Fire is connected to rajas and movement. It is an overabundance of tamasic energy that creates excess weight gain. If fire and rajas work well, this won't happen. Everything is interconnected. Whenever the consciousness of a particular chakra is out of balance, the corresponding part of the physical body is also apt to have problems.

Let's look at some examples of how differing elemental compositions will affect the shape and structure of the physical body. These are merely examples to help establish conceptual clarity and a working understanding of how the elements give rise to body structure. I'll use some extreme examples so the characteristics will be more obvious.

Short, dense people tend to have a predominance of earth element. Take this same short person and add on a bit of fat and curviness to the physique, and you have a predominant combination of both earth and water. Let's say this same short person was not overly curvy in nature, not fat, not gaunt or thin, but just healthy and trim looking; this would show a predominance of earth and fire elements combined. To contain a lot of fire, it is necessary to be robust, but fire itself will trim these people down so they won't have an overly water-based, curvy composition. Fire and water are opposite elements, as a person is very unlikely to have both of these predominant in their nature.

Let's now look at a very tall person. The tallness comes from air and ether elements. If someone is tall and thin, but still seems robust in nature, they are likely predominantly air and fire composition. Tall and thin, but weak and frail would show a predominance of air and ether elements. A person who is both extremely tall and very robust in stature, but not overweight or fat, is an example of where air and earth elements come together. Contemplate on these examples further to gain a greater depth of understanding. When one or two elements are not predominant it can be more challenging to identify elemental composition, but definitely not impossible.

Ether element can't be directly seen, but it can be felt. Have you ever met someone whose energy feels larger than life, or at least larger than their body should be able to contain? I'm not talking of powerful energy here, I'm alluding to a sense of people seeming larger than they can possibly be. It's subtle, but this is ether element. Since ether is also known as space, vastness is the attribute ether brings to people. Even if a person is short, if there is a large amount of ether element, they will feel energetically like there is more depth and substance to them than meets the eye.

Summary

In this chapter we've taken a careful look at both inner disposition (temperament) and body composition and how these relate to subtle energy of the gunas and elements. This is the basis of subtle energy that will impact your life the greatest as it forms who you are on a consciousness and physical level of being. You've had the opportunity to do two quizzes to determine the baseline of your own temperament and body composition and learned ways to deepen the exploration of what makes you uniquely you.

Part 1 of this book has covered the overall concept of vibrational healing, how it relates to the mind, heart, body, inner prosperity, and spiritual aspects of life. We've learned what subtle energy is and where it comes from. We've looked at the main chakras associated with overall health and discussed how the consciousness tied to each of these energy centers impacts the flow of subtle energy in the body. We've also looked at the subtle energy that creates overall temperament and physical composition through the gunas and the elements.

In part 2, we will discuss specific modalities for health and vibrational healing as they relate to both gunas and the elements. We will also learn specific techniques to practice for all of the gunas and elements. This will allow you to choose either temperament-based approaches (guna) to well-being or approaches based on your physical body composition (elements). Now, let's get to what you've been waiting for!

part two

Techniques & Tools for Healing

We've covered a lot of material on what subtle energy is, how it works, and what it can do as it relates to vibrational healing. We've discussed all of the pieces that go into creating temperament and physical constitution. Now it's time to start thinking about what vibrational healing approaches will work best for you. In the next chapters, we will take a careful look at how to use both temperament and physical constitution to determine what types of modalities will work best for you, as well as describe how these modalities correspond to guna and elemental composition.

Let's discuss some strategy for helping identify the best modalities for your current needs. It's necessary to be extremely honest with yourself; it's this self-honesty and deep self-inquiry that will point you in the right direction. The first question to ask yourself is "how do you relate to the world?" There are two approaches you can take. They are 1. elemental composition (physical energy type) and 2. temperament and guna correspondence (mind and spirit energy type). Both are related; they are merely different starting points. Do you relate to life more through physical sensory perception and direct experience, or through your ideals and sense of life purpose? If you relate best to life through sensory perception, which relates to your physical body, approach healing through the understanding of how different modalities relate to your personal elemental composition, which can be determined through the elemental composition quiz in chapter 3. This approach also works best when a person has no idea of their life path, purpose, or even what they really believe to be true. By working with the elemental modalities you can directly feel what works, what feels good to your body, and what makes the emotions and physical body stronger.

If you relate to life more strongly through your sense of ideals and life purpose (mind and spirit energy type), it is best to approach healing through the modalities that work directly with temperament and guna composition.

By determining the elemental composition, it is easy to determine the guna composition. Knowing the guna composition can then help in answering questions regarding overall life path and approach. You can also determine elemental composition by understanding your gunas and temperament, but this is more difficult. The basic difference in the two approaches is only in the starting point; in the end, everything merges into everything else. Temperament and guna-based modalities are elemental modalities and vice versa. I have discussed them differently solely because people relate to and understand life in different ways, either based on a bottom-up sensory-based approach or based on an inner-self-going-outward approach. After you have determined which approach will work best as a starting point, the fun begins!

Because each person is fundamentally different in temperament and physical constitution, everyone has a different starting point and way of approaching healing. If color is a medium that works best, then use color. If nature sounds work well, but not mantra or color, use nature! There is no right or wrong way to approach wellness—only what is best for a person based on their own unique temperament. Vibrational frequencies overlap in a person's temperament, making it possible for many different approaches to have a positive effect on health.

Another thing to keep in mind as you begin your journey of vibrational healing is to not have unreasonable expectations. Mental and emotional imbalances have to be given equal—if not greater—emphasis than the physical manifestation of a disease, because they are the primary cause of physical distress. Vibrational healing is not magic. It follows its own system of rules that have to be understood to make it work effectively. Follow the guidance given to you and diligently pursue your chosen modality; only then will it have the opportunity to heal and unlock you from the inside out.

Don't Forget about the Physical Body

While vibrational healing might appear to emphasize mental and emotional imbalances, that's only because the positive roles of mind and spirit are often neglected in conventional approaches to health. However, we must first and foremost pay attention to practical ways of taking care of the body. Since physical ailments are most often what cause us to seek healing, these items are worth noting up front as a foundational cornerstone to any vibrational healing modality utilized.

Exercise: It's stuck or stagnant energy that causes most physical problems. A large percentage of physical health problems would vanish through proper care and exercise of the physical body. How exercise impacts the body and what types of exercise are good will be different for everyone. Knowing your innate bodily structure, which is based on temperament and life purpose, can help in setting realistic goals for an exercise program. Exercise in this context is not about a specific goal, but in keeping the overall body fit through movement, which alleviates stagnation.

By keeping the body in good condition an overabundance of tamas guna and inertia are dispelled from both the physical and subtle energetic bodies. The less excess tamasic energy is present, the more energy will move freely in the body. Yoga is well-known in its teachings to target different ailments through specific yoga postures. Most of the postures are designed to bring breath, prana, and movement into stuck energy areas. Kundalini yoga and kriya yoga in particular are very powerful means of moving subtle energy in the body to correct physical health problems, but the intensity of these practices is not always well-suited to people who have severe ailments. Sometimes exercise is not possible due to a severe ailment, but when exercise is possible, do it. Prevention always works better than treatment.

Hydration: Even the act of staying well-hydrated by drinking plenty of water can assist in the healing process on a physical and emotional level. Drinking plenty of water helps to flush toxins out on a physical level—and whatever is happening on a physical level is also happening on an energetic one, since the two are intrinsically connected. Bathing or showering daily will also help. The feel of water on the physical body invokes a sense of cleansing and nourishment, which will trigger other positive feelings in the body. Have you ever dreamed of a nice, hot bath after a long, stressful day at work? The comfort water brings can make life more enjoyable when it is used consciously, with positive intention.

Positive Feelings: Since disease starts on an energetic level in the subtle body, working directly with the emotions can target disease manifestations before they ever reach the physical body. I cannot emphasize enough how important cultivating positive feelings is for overall health and well-being. When a person starts to feel better about life, life improves. Health improves. Spiritual connection improves. Energy flows more freely and health, happiness, and quality of life all improve.

Now let's take a look at various techniques and tools for vibrational healing!

Four

Healing Modalities
According to Physical Type
(the Elements)

· · · · · · · · · · · · · · ·

Introduction to
Elemental Healing Modalities

Let's take a look at some healing modalities and how they relate to a person's elemental composition. (*See quiz in chapter 3 for determining your elemental type*). When thinking about healing in terms of the body's physical constitution, there are two approaches that can be taken that often complement one another. One is to use a modality that a person has a strong resonance with: for example, if a person has a lot of earth element in their physical constitution, using an earthy modality such as aromatherapy as a way of working with that energy would be the way to go. The other way is to use a modality that corresponds to an area of the physical constitution a person is weak in, or having problems with. For example, a good approach for a person who needs to cultivate stronger focus and willpower would be a fire-related modality. A third way is to find a single modality that combines elements of both a person's strengths and weaknesses. If someone has both fire and air in their constitution, they should try the Pranayama Technique for Dissapating Negative Energy on page 201. How you approach this is completely up to you, and it will take practice to figure out what works best (or not at all). Everyone is different in both elemental constitution and overall disposition, so no one approach will work for everyone!

In order to work well with elemental modalities and understand the elemental constitution of a person, start with an evaluation of likes and dislikes. We've already discussed attributes of the different elements. Write each element down on a paper and some corresponding attributes for that element. For example, ether element would correspond to sound, music, voice, mantra, and anything related to sound or space. Once you have a list, rank each element from one to five with one being the element you are most favorably inclined toward. I recommend starting with a modality that you are very drawn to; something that sparks enjoyment and a sense of wonder. This will make the whole exploration of vibrational energy healing a positive and worthwhile experience, which is important because you are more likely to stick with and keep learning about things that you enjoy. Every modality takes a long time to truly deeply understand, so sticking with something is necessary to get to its depth. Let's begin the exploration with some modalities connected to earth element.

Here is a chart showing the basic attributes of each element.

Element	Sensory Perception	Attributes
Earth	Smell	Solid, rigid, fixed, contains all other elements within it.
Water	Taste	Flexible, flowing, adaptable, can take on vibrations of anything, cleansing, takes on the shape of any container.
Fire	Sight	Destructive energy to release subtle energy from its container to be used for other purposes.
Air	Touch	Lightness, uncontained, expansive, free-flowing.
Ether	Hearing	Subtlest of all elements, sound current, pure vibratory current that can create sound and light.

Earth Element Healing Modalities

Earth element has many, many modalities that are connected with it because earth element represents everything tangible and tactile. Since the physical body has a large earthy composition, there are many things from all parts of the world that correspond to making sure it is well-maintained. Working with earth element directly works on the physical body and can also work to bring balance to the root (Muladhara) chakra and the consciousness contained within this chakra, which relates to stability, solid foundations, and overall life purpose.

Other benefits to working with earth elemental modalities are their strengths in healing problems with the physical body. "Like attracts like"; oftentimes the denseness of the physical body needs something equally as dense to bring about a state of optimal well-being. By the time a disease state has penetrated the physical body, it needs to be treated with other physical, tangible things. For example, listening to a song might make you feel better emotionally, but it is not apt to heal a physical wound. Interestingly, since earth element contains the subtle essences of all of the other elements, earthy materials can impact all elements, senses, and even the emotions and psychological temperament directly. Earth element modalities are by far the most diverse, eclectic, and powerful healing modalities there are for working on all levels of the mind, body, soul integrated system. Because of this, we will spend a lot of time looking at some of the different modalities associated with earth element.

Aromatherapy & Essential Oils

Aromatherapy is a powerful modality related to earth element. Since it is earth element that governs the sense of smell, aromatherapy falls under this category. Smell is a primal sensory perception related to our most intuitive, instinctual self, and it also governs the sense of taste.

Aromatherapy is one of the many modalities that is extremely diverse and can have a combined effect with other elements and applications, with massage being an example. Oftentimes during massage, the massage oil base will have a particular fragrance that invokes balance within the body.

There are fragrances which work on each of the chakras, fragrances which work to balance emotions, mental disturbance, and much more. An in-depth practitioner well versed in aromatherapy can use the attributes of different fragrances to bring just about any body system, mental, or emotional imbalance back into harmony. Everything from aching muscles to headaches to nervous system pain to anxiety can be lessened through use of the right form of aromatherapy. Aromatherapy can be applied in many ways. Use of potpourri in a home is the most common example. The smell of a person's favorite dinner cooking can even be a type of aromatherapy because of the positive way it affects the psyche.

Essential oils are another common method and can be obtained for nearly any fragrance you want. Some essential oils can even be used internally as a dietary supplement, while many are meant for topical use or inhalation only. The benefits of essential oils are their potency and strong concentration. If you slice a fresh orange, the smell will be subtle. If you get an orange essential oil, the fragrance will be intensely concentrated and can then be used as a potent form of aromatherapy. Not everyone needs things to be so concentrated, so find what works best for you and contemplate as to why: this contemplation will help you better understand your strengths and weaknesses while overall better understanding yourself.

There are many well-written books, online videos, and other sources of information on aromatherapy and uses of essential oils. There are many companies that sell them in different grades of purity and therapeutic uses. Finding a high-quality oil brand to start with will show you what essential oils are capable of doing. Three of the most commonly used essential oils are lavender, peppermint, and eucalyptus. Lavender is touted as having potent antimicrobial effects and also works well for soothing anxiety and stress-related headaches. Peppermint will give a nice "pick me up" when feeling tired or mentally dull and is also a good headache remedy. Eucalyptus has some pain relieving qualities to it and is also known spiritually as a great purifier. This is just touching the surface of these to give an example of their uses.

Stones and Crystals

The use of stones and crystals is another extremely diverse modality that can be used to target any part of the mind, body, soul system. Like aromatherapy, there are many well-written books and guides to deepen your understanding of how to use them to bring balance to different parts of the body, thoughts, and feelings. The use of stones or crystals for people with a lot of earth element is apt to work very well because of the "like attracts like" phenomenon.

Stones, like the physical body, are dense. Earthy materials can more easily impact the vibrations occurring on a physical level.

Stones can be used in different ways. Their vibrations can be felt just by having them in a room with you, and this feeling is intensified when they are held or meditated with. Each type of stone or crystal has a different energetic vibration, so make sure to do some more in-depth research before starting an exploration of stone or crystal therapies. In addition to laying them on the physical body in some way, they can be kept in a pocket to keep their vibrations nearby or even used to charge a glass of drinking water. They can be applied directly on the body anywhere, including the chakra areas, to stimulate energy movement. Some stones will absorb energy out of a person, while some will emit energy into a person.

One of the most commonly used crystals is quartz, which has a variety of uses. Quartz crystals are very clear and hold a high energetic vibration. They can hold many vibrational frequencies inside of them and become a tool to facilitate diverse types of healing. For example, the energy of a mantra can be programmed into a quartz crystal so that it aligns itself with and emits the energy of the mantra it has been charged with. Quartz can also pull negativity out of the body, absorbing it into the crystal where it can then be energetically cleansed to get the negative energy out of it. Quartz crystal emits a high energetic vibration that helps to disrupt tamasic energy and promote clarity and overall well-being. Just having quartz crystals in a home or room can help to clarify the subtle energy in a space.

Hematite is an example of a stone used for grounding or earthing subtle energies. For people that tend to be spacey and flighty, hematite can help these people connect more here and now to the present moment. Many rocks and crystals including quartz can be cleaned energetically with both water and sunlight. There are some rocks that don't like sunlight, and some mineral-based rocks will dissolve in water, so it is important to research your particular stone before using it. There are literally stones and crystals for every purpose and many, many ways to use them in vibrational healing on a mind, body, and soul level.

Plants, Herbs & Spices

Many plants or parts of plants are well-known to have healing properties. A basic study into herbology or the use of spices in cooking will reveal tremendous insight into what plants can do. Originally, before there were synthetic drugs, chemists or herbologists would use plants as a way of healing disease. Plants have energies that can be used for a variety of purposes. Some (such as cloves) kill germs, some provide analgesic qualities, and some assist in rejuvenation. A common example of a rejuvenative plant is the aloe vera plant. Some have to be cooked and some are used raw, some topically and some through ingestion. It depends on the plant and the specific use. Aloe vera can both be used topically and be ingested to promote healing. On-ions, for example, can dissipate tamasic energy. Their raw form is very potent when ingested (think purple onions in salads), but their potency is not always as palatable to the stomach or taste as a cooked onion. Turmeric is an example of a spice whose potency is enhanced when cooked.

Cooking is often the most practical way that anyone can learn the medicinal benefits of plants. Cooking spices are commonly used as part of prevention and healing. Ginger root is an excellent example of a multifunctional plant and spice used in healing. Ginger can help alleviate an upset stomach, aid in digestion, and act to purify the body. Turmeric is another wonder plant. Science is starting to show all of the wonderful things turmeric can do, but spiritually it has been known for centuries to be a potent purifier, both inwardly and externally. It can be used to alleviate swelling and inflammation, and also to dissipate the energy of anger. It can wick negativity out of the body and help to clarify the aura. It can also be used on the skin to promote soft, flawless skin, decrease hair growth after shaving, and kill germs. Granted, turmeric will turn your skin yellow or orange, so it is best to be used sparingly—or with lots of soap! Using it as part of cooking is a good way to get its internal benefits and to help reduce inflammation in the body. The herb cilantro is often used internally for detoxification purposes. Cinnamon is used to heat the body, which helps prevent and eliminate stagnation. Cardamom does the opposite; it is cooling by nature and can be used to aid in digestion.

Plants and herbs are also commonly used in spiritual ceremonies to promote healing. White sage, for example, can be burned like incense to act as a purifier of energy within a home or confined space. The smoke acts like a broom to adhere to negativity and sweep it away. If you find plants or herbs to be of interest, deepen your exploration in this area. Plants can treat everything from a mental imbalance down to a physical disease manifestation, making them a very diverse tool in health and healing.

Time in Nature

Spending time in nature amongst the rocks, trees, plants, fresh air, and sunlight is a powerful way to rejuvenate the body, relieve stress, and cleanse the emotions. Nature is always nature, a tree is a tree, and a flower is a flower. There is an innate sense of self a person feels when spending time in nature that can be forgotten amongst the business of day-to-day life, where people often are not honoring their true essence. Since a tree doesn't know how to be anything but a tree, or a rock a rock, and so on, nature can teach us how to return to our most core essence and not try to be something we are not. Nature combines all of the elemental forces together, giving people exposure to every part of their own elemental composition.

Nature is also highly beneficial in two more ways to health and healing. First, being in nature provides a natural cleansing of the subtle energy in and around the body. Second, connecting directly with the earth is a means of grounding or earthing (both terms are commonly used) energy. Grounding enables us to better connect with ourselves and the rest of life in general. Just as electricity needs to be grounded to prevent problems, the energy in the body also needs to be grounded to prevent problems. Spacey energy or excess subtle energy in the body can overload the subtle body, causing pains and other physical problems. When energy is properly grounded, you will feel stable, free-flowing, and an increased sense of vitality and power, because grounding works so well to balance the flow of energy in the body. Grounding also provides a way to dump negativity and stress out of the body and give it directly to the earth. Since the earth is made up of decomposing material and contains the subtle essences of all the other elements within it, earth has a special capacity to absorb and neutralize energy; it can take in any energy and break it down into its source material. Just as excrement is used as fertilizer, you can give your BS and negative energy directly to the earth and it will use it as fuel to grow beautiful plants and flowers. *See "Visualization for Grounding Energy" in chapter 6 to learn a technique to ground your energy.*

A simple way to connect directly with nature is to spend time in it. Take barefoot walks on the earth. Feel the flowing water of a river on your hands and feet. Really take time to connect with what is around you and connect your energy deep with the heartbeat of the earth. Nature provides benefits on a physical, emotional, psychological, spiritual, and subtle energetic level of being.

There is not one aspect of life that spending time in nature won't improve!

Salt in Health and Healing

Salt is a great purifier. Salt absorbs water, and as such, it absorbs all of the vibrations contained in the water. By drawing in water, salt acts to purify whatever space it is in. For the body, a salt scrub can be used to exfoliate and rejuvenate the skin. An Epsom salt bath is recommended to draw pain, negativity, and stress out of the body. Even in the body, salt acts to cleanse and purify, and is an essential part of biochemical pathways, although salt should be used sparingly when consumed so as to not elevate sodium levels. Salts in excess are toxic to the body, so use them sparingly.

Spiritually, salt can be used to establish energetic boundaries to keep negativity out or positive vibrations in. It can be used to remove negative vibrations from a house or office space. A basic saltwater spray can be applied to the entryways of doors as a way to keep negative vibrations out of a home. By having salt around, negative vibrations get trapped in the salt and are then unable to mix with the energy in the body. You'll see evidence of this by spending time at the beach near an ocean. The saltwater of the ocean is very cleansing to the mind, body, and spirit. The salt pulls negativity out, and the water carries it away.

Since salt draws negativity out, its potency can be considered destructive. If salt is put on earth, for example, plants will not grow in that spot. Salt will kill grass if applied in excess. Destruction of negativity is a good thing, but too much destructive energy can also act to destroy that which is good and beneficial to life.

Water Element Healing Modalities

Over 70 percent of the physical body's composition is water element. All fluid in the body can be understood as part of water element. The fluids found within the body have two vital roles in life: to transport nutrients to all parts of the body and to remove waste products. The flowing nature of water allows for change, and change is a necessary ingredient in well-being. The body is always active—the heart always beats and the organs always function. For the body, stagnation is the enemy. Keeping things moving is the key to health, and water is a primary factor in keeping the body's systems balanced.

Water plays a vital role in well-being with all forms of vibrational healing. The fluids found in the body are a powerful container for subtle energy to move through. Water element carries positive healing vibrations throughout the body. Water is changeable by nature, and as such, can be charged with the positive and healing vibrations of many different things. There are techniques for charging water with the vibrations of stones, metals, mantra, prana, and other subtle energetic forces, which will be discussed shortly.

Water element is connected to the second chakra, which is considered the "abode of self." This makes the second chakra and water element very important for understanding and cultivating who an individual is. When water element is working to carry positive vibrations throughout the body, it becomes easier to stay in good overall health. When water element is full of negative vibrations, which can include thoughts and any negative belief an individual carries, this is the vibration being transported throughout the whole body, down to a cellular level. The body responds powerfully to the energy it contains.

Water element associated healing modalities help to get stuck energies flowing. Since water is connected to the emotions and feelings, water element modalities often work on an emotional level to facilitate overall well-being. Because emotions can be volatile, water related modalities should be approached with compassion toward oneself, as they can move stuck energies quickly and bring up a flood of trapped emotions. Feelings that are stuck in the body don't have the ability to express themselves until their energy starts moving, so when this energy is initially unstuck and starts to flow, a lot of negative feelings are apt to come up and be experienced before they are washed away. Once the energy remains unstuck, the emotions that were trapped in the stuck energy will go away. Water element modalities can be approached in a couple of different ways: working with the emotions directly or infusing water with the attributes of other things to help eliminate energy stagnation on a subtle level. Let's look at some techniques working directly with water.

Charging Water Element
with Subtle Energy Vibrations

Water can be infused with the vibration of just about any other thing, making it a dynamic conduit to bring different subtle energy vibrations into the body. Some of the most well-known examples of this are flower essences. The vibrational qualities of flowers are harnessed through transferring some of the vibration into a liquid. Even though none of the flower itself remains in the flower essence, the water contains its subtle energy, and as such, the attributes of the flower itself. This same concept is used in Ayurveda and other holistic practices where it is not possible or practical to consume the substance itself. For example, water can be charged with the vibrations of different gemstones, crystals, and metals. When a stone is worn or held near the body, the vibrations affect the body. When water is infused with their essence and then consumed, those vibrations can travel deeper into the body to help balance the body from the inside.

Subtle energy used in this way more often works toward altering the emotions and the mind, but through consistent use and finding the right energy to use can also work on the physical body. Water can also be charged with sunlight or moonlight to give it different qualities. A mantra or affirmation can be added to water by chanting the mantra while holding a glass of water or by touching the water directly while chanting. Mantra use will be discussed more in depth with ether element, but combining it with water can help a mantra work more quickly on a physical level. By combining a subtle energy with a tangible material such as water, the physical body itself is affected more quickly. Like tends to work with like; since the body itself has a high percentage of earth and water elements, earth and water element modalities work on the body quicker than the more subtle modalities of fire, air, and ether elements. Of course, oftentimes things we think are physical in nature stem from imbalances in other areas, but when there is something directly affecting the physical body such as a wound or visible problem, earth and water related modalities can act to correct the problem more quickly because these modalities are more physical in nature, just like the body itself.

Do some research to find the best way for you to work with modalities related to water element. When working with flower or herbal essences, it is best to obtain them from someone trained in the art rather than attempting to make them yourself. Charging water with mantra or with the vibrations of gems can more easily be done at home, but still requires some knowledge on the topic. For example, to infuse water with the attributes of gemstones is different than the process of infusing water with metals. If you want to learn more about this, delve into the particular area and learn from someone qualified in the art itself.

Oil Pulling, Sesame & Other Oils

Sesame oil has long been known as deeply healing oil to use in cooking, massage, and other applications. It is different from other oils in that sesame oil is believed to have the power to remove negativity from the mind, body, and emotions. Because of this, it is used as a base or part of a mixture in many Eastern massage oils. When applied to the body, it draws negativity out and neutralizes it. It can soothe basic aches and pains and act as a carrier oil to add other herbs to in massage.

One of the more esoteric applications of sesame oil is in its use in oil pulling. Oil pulling is discussed in Ayurveda, as are the overall benefits of sesame and many other oils, but oil pulling is still not mainstream or even commonly discussed amongst Ayurvedic practitioners. In oil pulling, a small teaspoon to tablespoon amount of unrefined sesame oil is placed in the mouth and gently pulled around through the teeth and around the gums for twenty to thirty minutes in the morning, before eating or drinking. It is then discarded in the trash, and the mouth is washed out thoroughly with mouthwash. It is important to not swallow the oil, as it contains toxins that have been removed from the body and trapped in the oil. The sesame oil acts to pull bacteria out of the entire body through the mouth. I'm not sure how it works, but its effects are undeniable. The cause of benefit has not been studied enough to determine, but one theory suggests it may hold benefit due to the tongue being connected to all systems in the body (just as in acupressure, the feet or hands both map to the different organ systems of the body, the tongue is similar). A consistent routine of oil pulling is said in Ayurveda to even be able to eliminate chronic, untreatable conditions. It will act on a mind, body, and emotional level to restore balance and draw out negativity. It also acts to whiten the teeth naturally and gradually strengthens both teeth and gums. Other oils including sunflower, coconut, and almond oil have been used in oil pulling, but sesame remains the most powerful option because of its ability to draw out negativity quickly and effectively. Sesame oil also has the ability to help remineralize teeth and help reverse small cavities.

Castor oil is another effective oil to use for massage, either as a carrier for other herbs or by itself. Castor oil has a heating effect on the body, and because of its low molecular weight is said to be able to easily penetrate the body, which has a positive effect on the deeper tissues in the body. Because it is heating, castor oil acts to move stagnant energy out of the body. Anything that is heating in nature lends a dynamic, moving energy that can help get slow-moving or stagnant energy flowing. Other oils as they apply specifically to massage will be discussed with air element.

Saltwater

Salt was discussed in its own section under earth element modalities. When combined with water, it can be used directly to draw negativity and stagnant energy out of the body. A good bath in Epsom salt will show you how well salts act to relax the body. Swishing with a saltwater mouth rinse or gargling with saltwater is also an effective means of cleansing the mouth. To take a natural approach, spend a day at the ocean if possible. Even just being in the salty air will act to purify the mind and emotions. Spending time directly in the water will draw stagnant energy out of the body itself. Think about the "beach bum" mentality—not a care in the world. Perhaps this is because of the cleansing effect of being near saltwater, in the sunlight, which is also greatly cleansing and communing directly with the earth. Try it for yourself and see how it acts to rejuvenate the soul.

Saltwater can also be used in the home as a purifier. Spritzing it on the baseboard of a wall will help to keep negativity out of a house. Spritzing it in the air periodically will act to dissipate any negative energy that has accumulated in a space without using incense or smoke, which can be disruptive to people with asthma or other breathing problems.

Fire Element Healing Modalities

As we have learned about fire element, it is connected with focus, willpower, and overall core empowerment. It has the ability to heat up and move stuck or stagnant energies. In the mind and emotions, it can eliminate negativity by burning away everything that is not serving a person's highest potential. Fire cleanses by eliminating the old and stagnant, which allows room for new growth, new thoughts, and new emotions. Just knowing that things evolve and change helps build confidence in life. It's comforting to realize that it is possible to add fuel to that which is good while burning away those things that are not positive. Fire is also connected with sight, which subtly is about both focus and perception.

When working with fire element, it is important to understand fire's connection to anger. Anger is a manifestation of fire element in the emotions. While it is not the only way fire can manifest in the emotions, it is an extremely destructive one. Anger energetically is almost pure fire, and as such, it is highly destructive. In addition to being fiery, anger is also directed toward a particular thing that has invoked the anger to begin with, making it very destructive toward the thing it is directed at. When a person who has too much fire inwardly does not direct it toward a positive expression, it can come out in the form of anger. Do not to mix fire with emotional or water-based modalities unless you really know what you are doing and have been trained appropriately in a specific modality that incorporates the two. An example would be doing simultaneous modalities that lead to deep emotional cleansing (like certain yoga or pranayama practices) combined with techniques that increase focus (like visualization or fire gazing techniques). Emotions need to clear out of the body gently and not build up to the point where fire ignites them, causing an emotional outburst. As far as the basic elements go, water will put out fire, or fire will boil water. Either combination does not work well. If too much fiery energy gets mixed in with the emotions, it is apt to lead to extreme emotional turbulence, anger, and negativity. Too many emotions nearly always dampen a person's focus and willpower. Fire in the emotions can lead to damage that cannot be quickly corrected. Let's now look at how some modalities related to fire element can help bring clarity and confidence into life.

Color Therapy

Color is connected to fire through the sense of sight. Working with colors can be a very positive way of working with the emotions to cultivate an inner change. Colors all have significance: even individually, colors will have a personal meaning. What I love about working with color is that you find it everywhere: in food, clothing, art, nature, and much more.

Let's look at the color orange as an example. Orange and shades of peach can work to instill a sense of creativity and vibrancy to life. You can work with this in so many different ways, as per your own inclinations. Painting a room a light peach color is a wonderful way to stimulate creative or artistic endeavors. You can eat orange foods and get some of these same effects. Peaches, oranges, carrots, orange bell peppers, and more will all work to bring nourishment to your creative energies. Even having artwork hanging on your wall that has predominantly orange hues will work to stimulate this energy inside of you. In cooking, you'll find a lot of orange in turmeric, which is known to be a greatly purifying spice.

Working within the spectrum of the color blue can have calming and cooling effects on the body. Sleeping with dark blue sheets can invoke a sense of relaxation in the mind and more restful sleep. Painting walls a light blue color in a bedroom would act to make the environment peaceful and regenerative. Blueberries have lots of antioxidant properties that aid the body in cleansing and purification.

Shades of green can be used to stimulate new growth in life and renew your sense of abundance and outer prosperity. You'll find lots of green taking walks in nature. You'll also find it in the kitchen through leafy greens, broccoli, salads, and more. Wheat grass, spirulina, chlorella, and hemp powder all range in shades of green and all provide a boost of energy and nutrition. *See "Technique for New Growth and Positive Change" in chapter 6.*

If you are drawn to artistic endeavors, work with the colors you feel attracted to. Contemplate their meaning in your life. Colors will help invoke different aspects of subtle energy into life and give you the ability to work with different types of energy. Just as sounds have different vibrational frequencies, so do colors. Find what works for you and deepen your exploration into its meaning in your life.

Visualization Exercises

Subtle energy will go where it is directed. What is in the thoughts or feelings will be amplified, because that is where the focus is. Even when thinking of something negative and not wanting that negative thing, energy goes toward the exact negative thing because thoughts are a form of energy. As opposed to focusing on what is not helpful, what causes fear or what causes pain, it is important to learn to focus on the things an individual does want to create—to learn how to add energetic fuel to the good and take it away from the negative.

Since thoughts lend much more energy to both problems and solutions than many people realize, learning to have control over where the mind goes is an important part of healing and overall balance. By learning to intensely focus energy on a particular area or thought, this thought will build in momentum. By focusing clearly in a healing practice, more subtle pranic energy will be directed toward the area to be healed. Meditation and visualization are opposite ends of the same spectrum. Meditation is about emptying the mind and consciousness of everything, whereas visualization is about laser-like focus on a particular thing. Each will act to strengthen the other, because they are opposite manifestations of the same energy. To empty oneself completely is a type of intense focus, and to focus on something intently is to empty the mind of everything else.

The reason intense focus is connected with fire is because it takes energy away from other things that would have normally received the energy that has gone into focus and intention. Also, the intensity with which something is being focused on creates a sort of friction subtly, which heats things up. Intense enough friction creates sparks, and these sparks ignite and burn things that have been cast aside. Things that are dead and decaying tend to burn better than things with a lot of water and life force in them. By pulling away energy from the old, the old paradigm of thought starts to die, which makes it a perfect fuel for the inner fire.

By cultivating a visualization practice, thoughts and subtle energy can be directed toward the creation of new thoughts and feelings. Visualization, in addition to being connected to fire, is also connected to the sixth chakra, the Ajna chakra. It is the Ajna chakra that helps in the process of creation of something new where the fire aspect of focus burns away the old. *See the numerous visualization exercises in chapter 6 for techniques to work with.*

Tratakum Practice

Tratakum is a type of focus-oriented practice used to connect you to the thing of your choosing. The most common type of tratakum exercise is to focus on fire itself. It can be considered a meditation technique, but its specific emphasis is on focus, not emptiness. This type of exercise is done by gazing at the flame of a candle. A flame will always flicker, even in a still room. This provides some insights into the nature of the mind itself. By learning to focus on the candle flame despite its constantly moving nature, it becomes easier to focus on other things, despite the constantly moving nature of life itself. Fire helps in understanding that focus does not require rigidity, but the ability to concentrate intently while allowing for movement and change to happen. This is an extremely important lesson for healers and in my opinion, for everyone in general. Healing itself is about change, movement, and intensity of focus.

Using fire for a tratakum practice will also help to strengthen the fire contained within the body. The external fire is merely a tool to cultivate that attribute inwardly. Increased fire inwardly can aid digestion, increase metabolism, and move stagnant energy. In the mind, fire will destroy negative thoughts and promote clarity. In the emotions, fire can clarify feelings and act to eliminate negativity, but too much fire will affect the emotions negatively, because emotions are of a watery nature. To use fire on the emotions, it is best if it is filtered through the mind and not targeted toward emotions directly. Think about the ways fire and water interact on a physical level: if fire is greater than water, fire will cause water to boil; just like what happens in a heated debate with someone. Too much water will put fire out. Make sure to use these two elemental modalities carefully, as they are opposite elements that, when paired together, can cause more damage than good. A tratakum exercise is not apt to trigger the emotions because it is working more on a consciousness and perception level than on a physical or emotional one.

Sacred Fire Ceremonies

In Eastern spiritual practices, the use of fire in ritual and worship is common as a way to invoke the attributes of fire inwardly. The same sorts of qualities that can be cultivated with a tratakum fire exercise can be cultivated through a sacred fire ceremony, although the effects of a fire ceremony are more far-reaching than a tratakum exercise. A fire ceremony normally includes the use of mantra and offerings into a sacred fire to ask for a desired result. As such, it is a combined modality that works on many levels of the mind, body, soul system.

For a spiritually inclined person, a fire ceremony can be tremendously beneficial as it works with belief and faith directly as a way to invoke positivity through fire. Invoking spirituality or God consciousness into water helps it to flow freely through the body. Invoking God consciousness into fire helps in cultivating focus, clarity, and destroying the things in life that don't take someone toward their dharma, or life purpose.

Sacred fire ceremonies can be used to cultivate a lot of energy very quickly; with the ability to then focus this energy, new things can be created and established quickly. Some Hindu and other Indian spiritual traditions have specific types of fire ceremonies called homa, homam, havan, and also agni hotra. With the faith component of a fire ceremony, which acts to eliminate doubt, results can happen even more quickly because there are fewer blockages in the mind. Fire ceremonies are an excellent example of the science behind spirituality as was more widely known in ancient cultures. Agni hotra works with the energy of fire directly, where homa or havan mixes fire with a specific prayer to God asking for a desired result such as prosperity, abundance, or removal of obstacles in life.

Sun Gazing & Solar Energy

Sun gazing is a controversial topic and also a practice that should only be done under guidance of a qualified teacher or guru. The sun is essentially a big ball of fire, but it contains within it all of the spectrums of energy in existence. Under normal circumstances, looking at the sun will cause damage to the eyes and can lead to blindness. Under appropriate conditions, however, sun gazing can be utilized as part of an overall spiritual practice to greatly increase the prana or subtle energy in the body, to clear negativity out of the mind, and to enable the physical body to heal more easily. There are stories of great saints who would subsist on the prana of the sun alone—without ever consuming food...only water. In more common application, it will reduce the need for food while giving a person more energy and focus in life.

Fiery energy and increased prana in general act to disrupt the density of tamasic energy, making people lighter, clearer, and more dynamic in nature. The sun is no exception. Since the sun contains all energies within it, its energy can be used to restore balance in all parts of the mind, body, and soul. Even just spending some careful time in the sun every day will help in building positive, clear energy. *See "Technique for Cultivating Mindfulness" in chapter 6 as a way of working with solar energy.*

Air Element Healing Modalities

Air element modalities help cultivate a lightness of being and include modalities that deal with breathing and the sense of touch. Touch is the physical sensation associated with air element. Exercises that build pranic capacity in the body often deal with air element. Prana is the fuel for healing; this energy has to be cultivated before it can be focused and dispersed in the body. *See "Visualization for Cultivating Subtle Energy" in chapter 6.* The greater a person's ability to cultivate prana, the more easily healing can happen both spontaneously and through directed focus. Working with air element modalities can heighten how a person relates to the sense of touch and can improve a person's capacity to direct the flow of subtle energy to different parts of the body. The ability to feel sensations is an intrinsic part of working with subtle energy. On an emotional level, touch shows us that we are not alone and can help cultivate a sense of inclusion and acceptance, both of which are needed to feel good and keep energy moving within the body.

Pranayama

Pranayama refers to breathing exercises used to cultivate increased prana in the body. Prana comes mainly from food, water, air, meditation, and the sun. Pranayama is used to harness the prana through breath and to direct this prana to different parts of the mind and body. Part of pranayama is in lengthening and deepening the breath; many people have very shallow breathing habits and don't take in much prana from the air, which means life force has to come from other sources such as food and water. A quick way to tell how efficiently you work with breath is to time your breathing rate, with the inhalation and exhalation equaling one breath cycle. An average healthy person will take fifteen breath cycles per minute. Needing to take more than fifteen breaths per minute is a sign that breathing could be made more efficient to increase prana within the body. Taking less than fifteen breaths per minute is excellent and shows the body is utilizing the prana that comes through breathing effectively.

During the process of meditation, the breathing slows down. During pranayama, the mind slows down and becomes more silent. The two are very interconnected; learning to lengthen and deepen the breath will help cultivate an effective meditative practice. After learning to deepen the breath, other types of pranayama can be learned that have specific effects, such as heating or cooling. There are practices which can strengthen fire within a person and exercises which can bring a cooling, nurturing effect. Other exercises focus toward breath retention or using the prana to transform stagnant energies within the body. After timing the number of breaths per minute, work toward consciously lengthening the breath to consistently reduce this breath per minute count. You might be surprised at how many things this can benefit, from a quieter mind to more steady emotions and an overall increase in energy.

Next, as you are breathing, look to see what part of the body is moving—is it the shoulders, the chest, or the abdomen? If the shoulders are moving, can you breathe deeper into the chest to make the shoulders stop moving? How far down in the body can you take the breath and does this change the way you hold your posture? It's all interconnected; the breath holds many secrets to how a person carries their body and how confidently a person can express himself or herself. Lack of prana creates fear in the psyche—just by cultivating deeper breath capacity the amount of fear in the mind can be decreased. Fear only happens when prana is absent. Something scary happens and it takes our breath away. Move through feelings of fear by bringing breath, prana, and the lightness associated with it into the mind, body, and emotions.

Increased control and focus of the breath can also reduce pain, as is seen in the breathing techniques associated with childbirth. How much of the pain reduction is due to focusing on the breath and not the pain, and how much of pain reduction is due to the increased prana breath brings the body? Breathing, like the flow of water or the flickering of a candle, reminds us that life is dynamic and changing in nature. Anything that acts to bring a moving energy into the mind and body will have an effect on thoughts, emotions, and overall well-being. *For practice, see exercises in chapter 6: "Pranayama Technique for Building Subtle Energy" and "Pranayama Technique for Dissipating Negative Energy."*

Massage

Massage therapy is great for relaxation, increased circulation in the body, and invoking positive feelings. Massage also integrates the use of oils, aromatherapy, herbs, heat, and even sometimes stones. It's a powerful combination modality that works with several elemental modalities at the same time. The sense of touch is one way we as humans connect to other people. Touch acts to relax the body and mind, lessening fear and promoting rejuvenation. It reminds us that we are not alone. Feeling alone can have a negative impact on well-being while feeling loved and supported can drastically positively impact a person's ability to heal.

By working directly with the muscles or fascia in the body, constrictions can be worked out on a physical level. Whenever physical constriction leaves, subtle energy will also flow. Massage also has a positive impact on the lymph system, helping to remove toxins from the body. When the right technique and right types of oils for a particular individual are used, massage can have a very positive impact on overall well-being. Since everyone's body constitution is different and we all relate to touch a bit differently, it is important to find a type of massage that works well for you and to find a practitioner that you feel comfortable working with. Some people will respond better to the overall relaxing feelings invoked while others may want a deep tissue or trigger-point massage to get into problem areas. Contemplating the type of massage you like, or if you don't like massage at all, will give you clues into your own constitution and character.

Reiki & Subtle Energy Healing

Reiki is a specific type of subtle energy healing that focuses on directing subtle energy from one person to another. Oftentimes this is done through touch, although it can be done without directly touching the body of another person. With enough focus and intention, it can even be done through distance. Reiki and other forms of subtle energies are often directed through the hands directly into the body of another person. The hands can be placed over the body, touching the air current between two people. In both a hands-on or hands-off approach, it is the sensation of touch that is affected. If someone puts their hand over a part of your body, you can feel heat emanating from it. This form of direct pranic transfer lends a very personal connection between the person giving and the person receiving energy. It can serve as a reminder that in life both giving and receiving are important for cultivating balance. In order for someone to give, another person has to be willing to receive.

Working with the energy of another person can help dislodge energy that we cannot directly see or feel on our own. Another person is not conditioned to our habituated responses or perceptions of life and often can see and feel things we ourselves are blinded to. Having this assistance in clarity of perception can help to target areas of the mind or body a person would otherwise ignore. Reiki and other forms of energy healing can also be done on oneself, which is advantageous if there is not another practitioner around or if a person wants to work with this healing modality daily. Another benefit of Reiki is that its energy does not have to be targeted toward a specific place in the body. It has an innate intelligence of its own that when this subtle energy is sent to a person it goes where it is needed within the body or mind to restore balance.

Reiki is an excellent tool for learning to work with and feel subtle energy. We all perceive energy differently; learning how you as an individual feel it will help in learning to cultivate it and direct it with intention throughout the body. For example, some practitioners feel injury or disease as a "hot spot" while others will feel it as cold and stuck. There's not a right or wrong approach; it's a matter of finding out how you perceive energy and states of imbalance. Reiki is easy and inexpensive to learn. Find a teacher who knows the art and take a day or weekend class as a means of getting started if you want to learn for yourself. Or just go and experience it as a healing modality from a trained practitioner.

Ether Element Healing Modalities

Ether element is what connects us to the sound current and the source of all vibrations. It is also known as space and is the building block that all other elements come from. All five elements contain the vibration and subtle essence of ether, making the use of sound related modalities a powerful tool for working on all levels of the mind, body, and soul. In its context of space, the openness and vastness of space helps remove clutter from the mind, expanding horizons and broadening perceptions.

Ether's connections to both sound and space are important in healing. Since sound has no density like the other elements (it's just vibratory current), it can disrupt the density in other things. It pierces through even solid matter (think earth) and can move out energetic stagnation to reestablish a healthy flow in life. As a note on pain management, increasing the amount of space in something will lessen its constriction. Pain comes from constricting or tightening something. When stagnation is removed and space is opened up, pain dissolves. Further contemplate this concept and ether element to deepen your understanding of how you can use ether element in your life to elicit positive change. Now let's look at some different modalities that work directly with ether element.

Mantra: Seed Syllables of Creation

Mantra is a powerful way of changing the subtle energetic structure of a person. When the subtle energy of a person changes, everything else will also change to reflect this new state of being. At the root of our essence is the soul and God. How well this inner state of conscious being shows itself to the world is solely based on what vibrations a person chooses to carry. Every thought, every feeling, and every sound in existence has its own vibration. The use of mantra, and in particular mantra containing *bijas*, or seed sounds, can have a profound effect on transforming a person's vibrations.

There are many bijas, the most common and widely known of which is "Om." There are thousands of mantras out there, most of which contain a combination of different bijas that work together to bring a specific effect. Bijas have vast power for making change. Sometimes a single bija mantra is used in meditation as a focal point to help silence the mind. A single bija can also be used to align the mind and consciousness with a specific vibration, including the vibration of a person's dharma. Bijas can also be mapped to the physical body and used as a form of mantra therapy for moving stuck subtle energies in the mind and body.

Chanting a mantra does not mean that the inner vibration will change immediately; what the bija represents has to be accepted inwardly and become a part of one's feelings for the vibration to integrate into all aspects of life. If a person chants a bija to cultivate inner prosperity, this person has to really want to be prosperous inwardly for its full impact to be expressed quickly. Through time, the bija vibration will work its way in and make a deep and profound change, even despite obstacles, disbelief, or lack of readiness. This is why it is extremely important to be careful about thoughts, words, and actions, because over time they will change a person's character just by making them a habit, for better or worse. Change can happen quickly when a person is truly ready to accept the change they are asking for, but the change will happen eventually with time and consistent practice.

A beneficial bija that anyone can chant in addition to Om is the bija "Srim" (pronounced shreem). It is a mantra connected to the spiritual heart, the seat of the soul, dharma, and all prosperity in life, inner and outer. It brings a positive calmness and sense of fullness to life that can act as a platform to accomplishing great things. Om dissolves everything into nothingness. Srim brings fullness and abundance to life, including the vibration of love itself. God is both fullness and emptiness, as is depicted in the Hindu conception of Shiva and Shakti. Shiva represents pure, still consciousness while Shakti represents this consciousness in dynamic motion, manifested through physical reality.

Longer mantras that combine bijas together can contribute to part of a daily spiritual practice to help change the mind and emotions to invoke positivity, healing, calmness, relaxation, and any number of other things necessary to connect with the soul and God essence within. Because of their ability to cultivate clarity, focus, and many other positive traits, working with a bija or mantra that is right for you can help to create a fundamental change in life that makes all of life better. Life always comes down to perception; things happen that we cannot change, but we can change the way we relate to life's situations. Working with mantra can help facilitate a change in perception that allows for obstacles to be more easily overcome due to cultivating a more expansive perspective of life.

When mantra is used as a means of therapy, a practitioner will use different mantras and bijas as a way of moving energy within the body. Thoughts and emotions get stuck in the physical body and using a mantra that works on a specific part of the body can help to get stuck energy moving. Overall, mantra therapy can be both relaxing and energizing, depending on the individual.

Singing Bowls

Singing bowls are an excellent option for working with sound vibration. Singing bowls come in different sizes and frequencies, and are made from a variety of different materials, including metals and crystal. They are actually standing bells; instead of a hanging bell that you ring, the singing bowl sits on a solid surface and you use a small mallet to vibrate the bowl's rim to produce the sound frequency. They can be played individually or in sets where the frequencies of the bowls complement each other. Singing bowls are used similarly to gongs to bring balance, increase the body's capacity to heal, and to aid in meditation and relaxation.

Singing bowls can also be used as a combined water and ether modality. Sometimes, water is put into the singing bowl as it is played, charging the water with the frequency of the sound vibration and the quality of the bowl itself. After a session of playing the singing bowls, the water is drunk or used to cleanse the body. The different metals and crystals have different energetic attributes: a copper singing bowl will give a different effect than a quartz singing bowl. You may find one works for you when the other does not at all.

This modality is one that can be very rewarding if you want to really dive in and explore sound frequencies and the effects of different elements on sound. It's one that with proper training, you won't grow bored with, because there is always a deepening into the depth of understanding of how this modality works. It's also a modality to give a fair try—if one type of singing bowl doesn't work, try another type that will give a different energetic response.

Using Words in Healing

Words are like mantras, with the main difference being normal words don't carry the same potency of creation a bija mantra does, but words themselves are combinations of vibrations that have an effect on the mind and emotions. Since words don't affect the root consciousness itself like a bija, words act as an affirmation. Affirmations can change the way a person thinks because they work on the positive nature of the mind, but it is important to believe what is being said. That is a difference between affirmation and mantra; an affirmation needs to be believed on some level to be effective whereas a mantra does not. Mantra has innate creative intelligence to it that works on a soul level whereas affirmation has only the intention we put to it through the mind. If the mind does not really believe an affirmation, its essence won't grow in a positive way.

Words affecting the mind can be both a positive and negative thing. People can become conditioned to believe things that are not true, just because someone said something. If someone tells you that you are ugly or worthless, this leaves an energetic impact on the mind. If it is repeated enough, a person starts to believe it. Does it make it true? Absolutely not, but it makes it a person's belief, which shapes their reality. When positive words are used that motivate and inspire people, people start to believe in themselves and their own inherent greatness. The great thing about words is that they only impact the mind for better or worse, but can never change the fundamental essence of the soul. Everything the mind learns can be changed with effort and practice in order to live the most positive and meaningful life possible. Words can fuel this or hinder this, so why not use them to make life more meaningful?

Words are a conduit for the energy they are being expressed with, which is why oftentimes people can read between the lines of what is being said and what is really meant. For words to hold their fullest power, intention and speech have to be the same—you can't say things you don't mean and expect your words to have a positive impact on yourself or others. When the words someone says deeply convey what is in the heart, words become a very powerful tool for teaching, healing, and motivation of self and others.

Inwardly, we as individuals can choose to change anything, but externally we cannot change others unless they want to be changed. This is why it is best to use positive words because if someone is hurt through the words we use, we don't have the ability to heal them unless the hurt individual accepts healing for themselves. Angry words are highly destructive and can leave lasting damage. The right words at the right time can inspire an individual for a lifetime. Are you using your words in the most powerful and productive way possible?

Music & Musical Instruments

Music can inspire just about anything. It can invoke any possible feeling within a person and change the way a person thinks. It can invoke relaxation, reduce blood pressure and heart rate, and slow the breath. It can also make people excited, angry, or stir the passion within. Since every other part of being has come from sound, sound will always have a primal impact on people. Because of music's ability to inspire and heal, it is often used as part of many healing modalities and in some cases is the modality itself.

There are two very powerful instruments, both of which are said to be able to re-create any vibration in existence: the gong and the didgeridoo. Both work to move energies in the body, restore balance, and facilitate an awakening of the innate healing capacity that is within every person. The beauty with musical instruments is they all have a personality of their own. The more an instrument is played, the more resonance can come from it. The deeper an individual goes into their exploration of music and a particular instrument, the greater depth they can find within themselves. An instrument provides a means of expression and an easy way to re-create myriad vibrations.

The voice is capable of doing the same thing, but again, it requires training and practice to get the voice properly tuned and capable of carrying a depth of feeling. Innate talent goes a really long way and with practice can turn into something great. Voice can be used as a means of healing, just as any other instrument, and voice can carry in it any vibration, just like the didgeridoo and gong.

Some instruments work well on particular areas of the body or mind due to the quality of the instrument itself. The flute is a good example of this. While it is definitely a sound-based healing modality, it is also strongly connected to air element. Wooden flutes are used in sacred ceremony and musical expression in both India and in Native American culture. Because of its connection with air element, and air itself making the resonance when in contact with the instrument, the flute can be very calming to the mind and emotions. Invoking a depth of calmness is sometimes all that is needed to facilitate healing in our overly busy world. When the body does not get adequate rest and true downtime, it cannot heal.

Drums are another very old and very powerful instrument to help connect to a primal healing vibration within. The sound of drumming has the innate ability to connect people directly to their heart and to connection with the entire world. Drums remind the being that life is a web and we are never, ever alone. Everything is interconnected. Good drumming can take the mind into a trance state where perceptions can be altered and healing can be invoked directly. It's a powerful way to consciously alter the mind and find connection with the whole.

Any musical instrument you feel a resonance toward can act to establish balance in life because of the enjoyment it brings. Any instrument can bring healing if that is the intention it is used for. To deepen an exploration of music and its uses in healing, contemplate what you like and why you like it. This will lend insight into what you are looking to cultivate and the best approach to pursue.

Star-Gazing

Star-gazing is one of the few modalities connected with ether element that does not involve the use of sound, but space itself. Spending time gazing at the stars and the openness of space itself can act to open the mind and expand one's horizons. Star-gazing works on opening the mind to new possibility and is also a peaceful way to relax and go within. Staring at the wide-open sky invokes a sense of wonder. What sorts of things do you contemplate when you stare at the open sky? How are your thoughts different than during the middle of a workday? Do you even make the time to sit with the universe, inwardly and outwardly?

When you look at the sky, what do you look for? Do you look for shooting starts and comets, or do you bask in the radiance of the moonlight and the twinkle of the stars? The moon itself is connected to our always-changing nature, and the phases of the moon can have a powerful impact on the psyche. Spending time with the changing moon each night helps to balance the different aspects of the psyche and emotions and can facilitate deeper healing on all levels of the being. When you spend time with the moon and stars, watch your emotions and thoughts. Watch how you feel about the moon and its changing nature. All of this will increase the ability of inner discernment to figure out what is going on in the subconscious mind and will help in facilitating growth and change.

Staring at space can also remind us that everything comes from the dark vastness of nothing. Everything was once nothing, and nothing eventually becomes everything. Spending time with the night can alleviate fears of the dark and fears of death while also deepening understanding of the process of life. Watch what feelings and questions come up and use them as a means of introspection.

Combination Modalities

We've already discussed quite a few combination modalities that use the effects of different elements in health and healing. Saltwater combines the elements of water and earth. Spending time at the ocean combines all of the elements together as the beach is earth, ocean is water, sun is fire, air is air element, and the openness of the sky is ether. Spending time in most parts of nature will combine its different elemental effects to balance the body, psyche, and emotions. Cooking utilizes spices, liquids, and herbs, all of which have a profound impact on the body and mind. Massage utilizes the sense of touch and very often uses oils, which represent water element, and herbs or fragrances that have an impact on earth element.

The more modalities that are combined, a deeper understanding of how they all impact the whole person is important. Combining modalities works well with integrated understanding and the more a person learns to understand the subtle ways all of the elements are interconnected, the more effective healing will become. If you as an individual know what it is that you need and what it is that you are, you can create a healing practice that will rejuvenate all levels of the being.

Beyond understanding how modalities relate to the elemental components of the body, mind, and emotions, looking at modalities that work in alignment with a person's temperament and life path can help immensely. In the next chapter we will discuss how to determine what types of techniques will work best for different psychological and emotional temperaments.

Five

Healing Modalities According to Temperament & Life Purpose (the Gunas)

············

Now that we've looked at how certain healing modalities relate to the elements, let's look at how some techniques and overall principles relate to the gunas and a person's innate temperament (see quiz in chapter 3 for determining your guna and temperament type). There is a lot of overlap, as the elements are a further distillation of the gunas, but learning how to target temperament can have a greater impact on overall life, confidence, and character development than just working on an elemental level.

When a technique or healing modality is targeted to work with a person's temperament, it has the possibility of unlocking a person from the inside out—removing the pin, so to speak, that creates problems in many different areas of life. Working through temperament is an excellent way to approach healing because it aligns a person with their core power that comes from the soul and place of unification with God and all that exists. To become truly linked with life purpose or dharma is a reflection of living in complete accordance with the positive manifestations of one's temperament and physical constitution. If a person becomes strongly connected to their dharma, all of life will correspondingly get better; inner prosperity increases, confidence is built, and the willingness to take chances in life and act in accordance with one's dharma, despite obstacles, becomes possible.

It's important to remember that it is the seemingly small things in life that often make the biggest impact. Life is far simpler than people know; taking the time to attend to the small details can have a huge impact on life. Small details set the foundation for life upon which everything else can be built.

Healing Modalities that Work with Sattva Guna

Sattva guna is important to cultivate within one's temperament for two main reasons. Sattva is required to have clarity of one's life purpose and path, and an individual's dharma, gifts, strengths, and weaknesses. Without having clarity of these things, life is confusing and a person jumps from one thing to the next seeking fulfillment. Since fulfillment comes only from living life's purpose, this clarity must be cultivated. Second, sattva is the sustaining energy of the three gunas. Rajas acts to create, tamas either solidifies or destroys, and sattva sustains what has been created. Without cultivating sattvic qualities, it is impossible to fully live life's purpose or to maintain overall good health. Good health and positive lifestyle comes out of being able to maintain all of the inner prosperity that has been dreamed of and created in life.

Silent Meditation

The primary way to work with sattva guna is to have a regular, consistent meditative practice. And specifically to work with sattva, it should be a meditation that is silent and takes you into the core of your being, not a technique that trains the mind. Meditation techniques are active and work with different parts of the body whereas silent meditation uses no more than a single bija mantra as a way to still the mind and enter into silence. Meditation techniques act as precursors to help people silence the mind long enough to be able to enter into a place of actual meditation and stillness. Most people find it very challenging to sit and meditate effectively; more often than not, this ability to sit calmly comes as a result of persistent effort and first starting with other techniques and modalities to appease the body, emotions, and the mind.

Even though feeling like you have an effective meditation is challenging at the beginning, it is important to sit and do it anyway. The consistency will lead to anything becoming effective. The problem most people face is in giving up too soon. With meditation, success won't come easily or quickly; patience and acceptance is needed. There are no quick fixes to life, and meditation is a practice that teaches these difficult lessons. Even just a few minutes in silence can have a dramatic impact on life contributing to stress relief, lessened anxiety, and an increased sense of inner peace.

When these big obstacles are removed, more inner clarity can come to the surface. Clarity can be likened to a spontaneous rising of inner awareness and intuitive capacity as it applies to one's own self. It's always there—it's normally just buried under the louder voices of stress, pain, emotional fatigue, depression, and any number of other things. The really awesome thing a person will learn when they develop a consistent daily routine, even if this routine is just for fifteen minutes a day, is how even small amounts of time consistently put toward a practice will yield tangible results. If you meditate every day, you will see changes within a few months' time, if not within a few days' time.

Clarity gives rise to all good things in life. This place of inner silence is also what brings about the capacity to respond to life instead of reacting to it. When you feel your own essence, everything else comes to a place of peace. How meditation relates directly to sattva guna is in its ability to awaken a state of clarity and cultivating the capacity to maintain it. It's the craziness of life that takes us away from what we really are that causes turbulence. Isn't getting a deeper sense of who you really are and cultivating the capacity to actually live it worth a few minutes a day?

Visualization Techniques

Visualization can work with either sattva or rajas guna, depending on the result a person is trying to accomplish. Cultivating the capacity to visualize helps in sustaining a desired state of being and this sustaining aspect of life is related to sattva. To sustain something, it must be under a person's control. The capacity to control that which is within comes from both the clarity related to sattva and the focus related to rajas, both of which work through the sixth chakra. For sattva, cultivating the capacity to visualize strongly will help in maintaining the clarity that arises from sattva and meditation. If clarity is not maintained, focus on a particular goal cannot be maintained either. Lack of clarity leads to lack of focus, and lack of focus does not allow anything to be maintained or sustained.

The stronger a person's capacity to visualize something, the easier it becomes to use this skill to focus on anything. Visualization can be as simple as trying to visualize oneself inwardly and feel the different parts of the body. It can be focusing on visualizing a sacred geometrical design and holding the image in the mind as long as possible. It can be as complex as visualizing oneself doing something specific and attaining a desired result. Since it is the energy a person vibrates within that acts to shape reality, a person can only attain in life that which they have the capacity to dream of or visualize. If it doesn't come into even one's thoughts, how can it become a reality? The more a person can visualize what they want, the easier it becomes to get what they want because the energy is no longer foreign; it becomes familiar and comfortable and enters into feelings (and as such, ether element) directly.

On a more tangible level, when a person takes the time to focus on something it is obviously something that they really want. If a person really wants something, they will be willing to work for it. Cultivating clarity of what is truly wanted in life gives fuel to the desire to actually attain it. The clearer the focus and capacity to visualize, the clearer the desire to attain and sustain the goal will be. Visualization and meditation work in tandem to cultivate and sustain whatever it is a person really wants. Without being able to focus, life becomes a process of constant creation and destruction, moving from one desire to the next. Cultivating sattva in one's temperament works directly on teaching a person how to start shaping reality according to one's dreams and how to sustain this reality once dreams have been made a reality.

Healing Modalities that Work with Rajas Guna

Rajas guna is responsible for the creative aspects of life. It is the aspect of our temperament that gives enough fire, drive, motivation, and desire to accomplish anything.

Rajas energy is dynamic and always moving. When learning to work with this energy, a person gains the ability to work diligently toward goals, to create a desired effect, and to have the sheer desire required to want to make something a reality. Let's face it. If you don't really want something, you won't be willing to put in the desired work. This directly connects with the mental and emotional aspects of life, but it also connects to the physical body because of the energy rajas brings. Without physical energy and willpower, nothing would get done. No actions would take place, and the body would remain in a state of inertia. Rajas is the key to working effectively with both the sattvic traits a person has and the tamasic ones. Rajas is the pin; without willpower and drive, dreams would never be brought to fruition. It's the majestic, capable, and royal aspects of a person's temperament. It also takes a lot of work to cultivate properly because self-empowerment means being willing to acknowledge and work through weaknesses—physical, mental, or emotional. Health is not possible without being willing and able to work directly with one's own self.

Meditation Techniques

Silent meditation works primarily with sattva guna, but meditation techniques work primarily with rajas guna. In a meditation technique, there is an aspect of either visualization, pranayama, mantra, or some focal point that is not stillness or silence itself. Techniques are used to train the mind and emotions to respond in a certain way. Techniques help to break unwanted tendencies and cultivate new, beneficial ones in their place. An effective meditation technique will work to slow the mind so that it can learn to focus on a desired objective.

Some techniques work to bring more prana into the body. Some work to silence the mind. Others work to teach the mind to do something specific, like visualize more effectively. Regardless of what a technique is being used for, it is preparing the mind to eventually sit in a place of silence. Until the mind can be controlled, it cannot be silenced. While a lot of people would call a meditation technique merely a meditation, I call it character development. Techniques cultivate the capacity to accomplish whatever you want to in life, and they teach through experience the required work and focus required to be successful with anything in life.

The skills cultivated through meditation can be applied to all parts of life. Staying consistent, working hard, and keeping your focus in one place are three traits are required to have a good life and to have a healthy life. Before a person can live these attributes successfully in outer life, they must be cultivated within. Working with a meditation technique will help facilitate this process of confidence-building so that a person knows they have the capacity to be both successful and healthy in life.

Healing Modalities
that Work with Tamas Guna

Tamas guna is both the most easy and most difficult guna to work with. It is easy because all it requires is that a person gets up and does something in life. It's difficult, because to do the right things requires both clarity and willpower, which are a result of working with the sattva and rajas gunas. Any healing modality that works with earth and water elements will work well with tamas guna. To approach tamas from a temperament standpoint, one must learn to understand the constantly dynamic nature of life itself.

Since tamas guna lends itself to inertia, stagnation, and overall confusion in life, it can be very difficult to break free. The average person won't know exactly what needs to be done in order to live a perfectly healthy and balanced life. This is normal. What can be done is to cultivate trust in the process and to always stay active and engaged with life. While I can't recommend a specific technique or modality for this, I can recommend that people work to engage themselves in this present moment with everything life has to offer. Learning to be mindful of what is happening is a great start to this process. *See "Technique for Cultivating Mindfulness" in chapter 6.*

Life itself is the greatest of all teachers. If a situation happening in life is not beneficial for health and well-being, it is possible to change it. This is the power that tamas guna has—nothing is permanent. Everything that has become manifested in life is transient by its very nature. Feelings come and go. Jobs come and go. Relationships come and go. Nothing stays the same forever. Life is constantly evolving into something else. It can move in a productive way where goals and dreams are being created or it can move in a chaotic way that disrupts goals, dreams, health, and overall well-being, but everything is always moving and changing. By entering into this flow of life, a person can engage with tamas guna directly.

Physical activity is an excellent way to train the body and mind that activity is essential for all things in life. Yes, some people literally spend their lives sitting on a couch, watching TV, playing video games, eating, sleeping, and doing little else. Remember, when inertia sets in to the body, it will also set in to the mind and emotions. To stay receptive to life and what is happening in each and every moment, stay active. Activity and cultivating rajas guna are the only ways to step out of inertia. Meditation does not work well on tamas because it is too much like tamas. Both quiet the energy, and a tamasic person needs to get moving, not to quiet stagnant energy.

Exercise daily. Eat a healthy, balanced diet. Contemplate life in general. Work toward accomplishing dreams and have productive hobbies. All of this will help to keep tamas guna being a benefit to life and not a hindrance. In fact, anything including all of the techniques for all of the gunas and elements will impact tamas guna. This is all practical advice; nothing heady or intellectual need be said about tamas. Just get up and do something in life, even if you don't know if it is the right thing or not! If it's not right, you'll eventually learn what is through the process of trial and error. Cultivate stagnation, sloth, and inertia and all of life, including physical well-being, will reflect this. The more stagnation is present, the more basic the advice of what to do to solve the problem: proper diet, exercise, and rest. Nothing else can really be done until these things are brought into better balance.

Be willing to get up and do something and you can live your life's purpose. Take some chances in life and really live. Remember that tamas guna serves as the foundation for life. If it is being neglected, everything in the mind, body, and soul complex will suffer. If it is being used to cultivate proper rest and proper maintenance of the body, everything else will become possible.

SIX

Techniques to Practice
for Health & Healing

· · · · · · · · · · · · · ·

We've now looked at the different gunas and elements and discussed their attributes. You've had a chance to contemplate on what your own constitution is and now you're ready to get started trying some techniques on your own. I've outlined a few effective techniques for you to work with that will help you promote healing, center and balance your energy, and stay positive as you continue on your journey.

A Note on Working with Techniques
These techniques that have been presented will give you a well-rounded toolbox to start your journey with. Learn how they work together and what works best for you. Continue exploring other modalities as they fit your unique

temperament. Here are some things to keep in mind as you move forward.

Consistency in doing a technique is more important than the length of each session. For example, it is better to do a technique consistently for six weeks for five minutes a day than to do it three times a week for an hour. Doing something daily impacts the mind more strongly, to the point that it settles into the subconscious mind and becomes a natural process that doesn't require extensive focus. Over time, the mind will start to do the technique without you even thinking about it. Each technique has a range of time associated with it for best results (for example 4 to 12 minutes is common), so pick what you can do consistently each day and stick with it. If consistency is an issue, pick a shorter duration and gradually work up to a longer duration. Techniques are all about reprogramming the mind to have positive lifestyle habits. Take advantage of the way the mind works—who really can't commit five to ten minutes a day to health and well-being? In addition to the specific benefits of the technique itself, you'll notice things changing in other areas of life too, because any time you can learn to be consistent with one thing, it simultaneously strengthens many other areas of your life.

Keeping a journal is a good idea because by briefly documenting your experiences after completing a technique every day, you can watch how you change over time. After doing a technique consistently for at least three weeks, see how it is changing you. See how it's changing you after six weeks, six months, and so on. The most important thing to remember is this: if a technique works, keep doing it. Don't stop just because you feel better! Keep with the routine as a means of preventative maintenance and you'll find yourself staying healthy, as opposed to working with subtle energy to recover from an illness. Each time you practice a technique, you are putting a little bit of energy in your inner savings account, which you can get out and use when it's needed. Your inner savings account and inner prosperity are linked—don't let either become depleted!

Lastly, give yourself adequate time with each technique to really assess if it is working for you or not. If the technique seems like it is not working, it may just be pushing up against your own limitations and inner pain and actually be doing precisely what it needs to be doing. Be honest with yourself. Be introspective and look deep within. Your healing journey will require you to smooth out the rough edges of your character, so as to find that place of balance within yourself. Let yourself be polished and scrubbed when necessary so as to find the pearl you are looking for. Health, wealth, and happiness of all kinds require you to act in accordance with your innermost nature. See where the techniques help you do this easily and where they rub you the wrong way. Both sorts of rubbing will be necessary to find your true essence.

Visualization for Grounding Energy
(fire, earth, and sattva)

Just like electricity works best and is safest when it is properly grounded, subtle energy in the human body works best when you know how to ground yourself. Grounding has two main effects: it promotes energy movement in the body and it eliminates excess subtle energy. Both help in staying balanced and opening up to stronger healing vibrations. Grounding can also be used to remove negative subtle energy, negative thoughts, and any unwanted subtle energetic vibration. When the body stays grounded, you are capable of receiving and moving more subtle energy than you are when you are not grounded. Grounding in terms of the body refers to a process of fully connecting with the body and with Mother Earth herself.

When you ground yourself or a specific energetic vibration, you are giving it to the Earth. Don't worry, the Earth uses it all—even the vibrations we consider negative. Remember where fertilizer comes from. What is excrement to one thing becomes fertile ground for another. The Earth takes all of it and transforms it into neutral energy that becomes the foundations for all of life. Here is a technique to ground excess or unwanted energy.

Sit in a comfortable position, either in a chair or directly on the ground. If you can sit outside in fresh air, all the better. If not, the technique will still work just fine. Living in Minnesota for a few years taught me it's not always possible to go outside and get some fresh air, especially when the temperature is -20 degrees F and your nose hairs freeze instantly. Get comfortable wherever you are so that you can truly relax. Just make sure you feel the ground, either by sitting on it or with your feet. Close your eyes and take a few deep breaths in and out. Breathe in the air around you, becoming aware that air carries in it lots of subtle energy. Breathe and bring this energy into the body. Visualize this extra energy swirling around inside of all parts of your body, paying extra attention to any areas of disease or pain. Visualize roots from your feet or sitting bones extending down into the earth; dense, thick, brown, earthy roots. Extend them down several feet into the earth. Feel the earth drawing your subtle energy into it. Let it take all of this extra energy that you are breathing in and swirling through your body and chakras, pulling it out of your body and dispersing it deep into the earth like fertilizer. Once you are done, visualize the roots reabsorbing into your body, but remain connected to the vibration of the Earth, knowing you can reconnect with it anytime you want to. This technique can effectively be done in as short as 3 minutes and for up to 12 minutes per day. Anything beyond 12 minutes is not necessary. Take notes each day of how the technique makes you feel and how it is changing you, if its effects are gradual or rapid. This will help in your self-inquiry while pursuing your healing journey.

Visualization for Cultivating Subtle Energy (fire, air, and sattva)

Now that you know a good technique for moving your subtle energy and grounding it so that more can come in, let's learn a technique to cultivate more subtle energy in your life. It's important to know how to ground first though, because bringing in more energy when you don't know how to ground what you have can be overwhelming for some people, depending on the type of energy you are looking to cultivate. Subtle energy can be cooling, heating, or energizing in nature. The way in which it comes to you will give you clues to your temperament. This is a technique to connect you with the energy of the sun. The sun contains all spectrums of energy, so you can get from it exactly what you need. Even if you don't know precisely what you need, it will work to balance your energy and fill in gaps as necessary. It may be strange to think the sun also contains cooling, healing energies, but it does!

It's best to do this technique either in the morning or during the day, because the energy of the sun will get energy moving inside of you, and this activity may make it difficult to sleep. Go outside and feel the rays of the sun on your skin. Take time to notice how it feels. Connect yourself with the energy of the sun by feeling it on you and inviting this energy into you. As you feel the energy of the sun on your skin, visualize it entering into your body and moving through all parts of the body. Keep inviting it in. Visualize the energy moving out stagnation and balancing areas of disharmony or disease. Tell your body to take what it needs from the sun, and to leave the rest behind.

Go outside and bask in the sunlight for a few days or weeks as necessary until you really know this feeling of the sun on your skin. Once you know how it feels, you can do the technique anytime, anywhere, even if you are not directly basking in sunlight. You can invoke the feeling and vibration directly from inside of you, because in your own subtle energy you carry the energy of the sun. Do this for anywhere from 3 to 11 minutes, depending on how much you feel the energy. If you feel it quickly, keep the visualization to 3 to 5 minutes. If it is more difficult to connect, do it for up to 11 minutes.

Meditation Technique for Cultivating Healing Energy (fire, air, sattva, and rajas)

There is a difference between deeply meditating, which is you listening to your soul and God, and working with a technique. A technique helps the mind to focus and direct energy, which requires it to stay active (rajas energy). Deep silent meditation (sattvic energy) is the exact opposite; it goes beyond the mind once the mind has reached stillness. A technique can be an effective gateway to silent meditation because you slow down the mind with the technique, which makes it easier to then sit in silence. In deep meditation, you become open, expansive, and empty. Let's learn a technique that will teach the mind how to cultivate healing vibrations inside of your body and make it easier to reach a place of deep meditation.

The place of health within is strongly connected to balanced energy; we have both hot and cooling energy that runs through the body. Too much heat disrupts, too much cool keeps things stagnant. Sometimes the difference in these energies is thought of as masculine versus feminine, but regardless, they are opposite polarities that need to come together to be most effective. Find a place where you won't be disturbed for a while. Get into a relaxed seated position and sit quietly and close your eyes. Take some deep breaths in and out and visualize a combined midnight blue and white light coming into your body. Visualize this energy entering into all parts of the body, bathing you in total balance, healing, and grace. Try to feel the distinctions between the white light and the blue light. Feel them united as one and as separate energies, working to bring everything into balance. Focus this energy everywhere, but add extra emphasis to any parts of the body, emotions, or mind that need extra healing. At the end of the technique, sit in absolute silence for at least 5 minutes where you are not visualizing or thinking anything. You can sit in this silent place as long as you want or are able to. Just let yourself bask in the energy you have created or in the concept of nothingness itself.

Work with this technique for between 6 to 11 minutes a day, plus the silent portion at the end, and do it consistently. It can be done day or night with no adverse effects.

When intense heat and intense cooling come together as one, the energy will be felt in interesting ways. Delve into this experience and see how it makes you feel. See in your visualization how the color of blue changes as it combines with white light. It will take on a different shade than the midnight blue you start with. The blue light is representative of the cooling, feminine energies. It's the universal void that everything else comes out of, including all light, all energy, and all brilliance. It's the potential energy of creation that has the ability to dissolve disease and reabsorb it back into pure neutral potential energy that can be used to create new beneficial things in life. The white light represents the culmination of purity and light that comes out of this void, the luminous inner being and God force that is born from the potential consciousness itself. It's hot, fiery, and pure. White hot, in fact. The two together as one destroy negative energy and help it to reabsorb back into its source. It brings the mind, body, and emotions back to a place of unity and balance. Health care symbols to this day are often still depicted with blue and white. Delve further into the symbolism of these colors and the history behind them if this is of interest to you.

Pranayama Technique for Building Energy (air)

Lots of subtle energy comes from the air we breathe, so working directly with the breath in different ways can draw more subtle energy into the body. If you want to learn more pranayama techniques, this is an active part of most yoga asana classes. There are techniques for heating, cooling, relaxation, focus, and just about anything you can want. Let's learn a technique to help you build energy.

Sit quietly in a comfortable position. Take a few deep breaths in and out to start getting relaxed. Close your eyes so you can more easily focus solely on your breath. Inhale deeply in an 8-second count with steady breath the entire time. Essentially, it should take you 8 seconds to completely fill yourself with air from the breath. Once you have inhaled completely, hold your breath for 4 seconds. Exhale all of the air in a 4-second count. When you are ready, repeat this cycle 21 times so that you complete 22 total breath cycles. If you don't want to time the count, that is fine; just count to eight in a steady rhythm and keep the same rhythm while you count to 4 for holding and exhaling the breath. Once you have completed 22 breath cycles, take a few normal breaths and smile before going back to your day.

Having a longer inhalation than holding the breath and exhalation helps in cultivating your body's capacity to contain more subtle energy. Illness always results from stagnant or depleted subtle energy, so techniques like this can help revitalize the body. This will take you less than 10 minutes a day and can be done anywhere.

Pranayama Technique for Dissipating Negative Energy (fire and air)

This technique is opposite from the one above and helps train the mind and body to detoxify itself by focusing attention on the exhalation rather than the inhalation. Sit quietly in a comfortable position and close your eyes. Take a few deep breaths in and out to relax before starting the technique. Take a deep breath in a 4-second count. Hold the breath for 4 seconds (or a four-part count). On the exhalation, exhale for 8-seconds; this means the breath should be measured so that it takes you eight full seconds to fully exhale all of the breath you have inside. Again, if you don't want to time this, you can use an 8-second and a 4-second count inwardly as long as you keep the same rhythm for the technique (your 4-second count should be half as long as your 8-second count). Repeat this breath cycle 21 more times for a total of 22 total breath cycles. Once you are done with the technique, take a few comfortable breaths in and out and remember to smile before going back to your day.

Anytime you work with the breath, it can be normal to get a bit dizzy or disoriented. If the body is not used to taking in extra oxygen and subtle energy, it can take some time to get used to this. Notice it with this technique and the pranayama technique for cultivating subtle energy and determine which one feels the best to you and gives you the best results. This will tell you a bit about your character. If you prefer the technique to cultivate subtle energy, working with your inner prosperity and sense of abundance will be a tremendous asset in your healing journey. If you prefer this technique to dissipate negative energy, working strongly with inner discernment, then contemplation and destructive types of practices, such as those dealing with fire element, will most likely be extremely effective for you. If the mind knows there are things it needs to get rid of, you'll be inclined toward dissipating and destructive techniques. If you feel empty and need inner nourishment or love, the cultivating techniques will bring this into balance.

I enjoy working with both. When I started my journey, I was very fond of the dissipating and purifying techniques and I have always loved fire. Later on in my journey, I gravitated more toward the sense of fullness. I now use both depending on what is needed in the moment; some days it's good to dissipate energy if there has been a lot of stress or discord. Other days it's good to focus on cultivating positivity!

Mantra-Charged Water Technique (water and ether)

We've discussed the importance of water for carrying vibrations and its power to assist our healing journey. Let's learn a technique to infuse a glass of drinking water with the positive vibrations of mantra. Mantra-charged water can give an extra positive boost to the vibrations you experience during the course of a day, leading to more positive emotions, feelings of personal empowerment, and greater overall happiness.

Take a glass of drinking water. Hold it between both of your hands with the palm of your left hand holding the bottom of the glass and the palm of your right hand holding the top of the glass. Visualize and try to feel your connection with the glass and with the water inside of it. Take yourself back to the memory of a very positive experience in your life, so as to get these positive vibrations flowing through your body. As you hold the glass, say the bija mantra "shreem," and repeat this several times. Shreem is a bija mantra of beauty and fulfillment of the heart's desire, so it is a positive one for everyone to work with. Its energy is gentle in nature and tends to evoke feelings of love and joy. Make sure to really chant the mantra and make it audible! Feel the vibrations of the mantra pass through your hands and into the water in the glass. Shreem will help in cultivating stronger feelings of inner prosperity to help in all aspects of life.

Once you have chanted the mantra a few times, drink the water in the glass. It now carries this vibration with it, and this vibration will travel with the water into the body to provide subtle energetic nourishment on a physical level. You can charge water with any mantra you want or even use an affirmation in its place if there is not a mantra you feel comfortable working with. The important thing is that you feel the positive vibrations of what you are saying being transferred into the water. Ensure that you have a personal connection with whatever mantra or affirmation that you use. This will help the technique to work on a deeper level of being.

This technique is extremely fast and can be done as often as you want. I always bless my water with a mantra before I drink it. This is similar to saying a prayer for blessing over food or drink. If you want to notice a difference in your life from this technique, do it at least once every day, and more often if you can.

Gemstone-Charged Water Technique (earth and water)

Perhaps you don't feel that mantra-charged water is right for you at this time, but you still want to get the effects of charged water in your life. Or perhaps the message you want to convey to your body and spirit is more complex than can be guided through a simple affirmation. Working with gemstones is an excellent option. Gemstones all carry specific and complex vibrations to them that will work on different levels of the being. The other nice thing about working with stones is that they don't fluctuate in their consciousness in quite the same way we do. You'll be able to get the exact vibration you want from them consistently. Just as with mantra-charged water, gemstone-charged water can increase positive emotions and feelings of greater empowerment and happiness.

Make certain that you clean your gemstones with water before using them and use a stone with a vibration you want to take into your body. To help choose a stone, consult one of the many excellent books and resources about the vibrations of stones and crystals. Wash your stone thoroughly with hot water, then rinse it in cool to cold water. Some gems love to be purified in sunlight, and others in moonlight, in addition to their cleansing in water. Do some research on the stone you are using before you use it to charge your drinking water.

Once your stone is adequately cleaned both physically and energetically, place it in your glass of water and leave it there for at least 11 minutes. Eleven is a number of mastery and working with its vibration will help add mastery to your life. You could leave it longer if you have the time, like overnight if you want to, but this is not necessary. Make sure to remove the stone from your glass before drinking the water. You could also consider putting your stone in a pitcher of stored water, so as to not have to do this with each individual glass of water you drink. Just be sure to wash the stones each time your pitcher gets empty before you add more water to it.

My birthstone is peridot. Peridot has many attributes that work on a spiritual, emotional, and physical level. By adding my birthstone to a glass of drinking water, I am working with a stone that already has a natural inward resonance with me, which makes its impacts more strongly felt in my life. Another way to select an appropriate gemstone for you is to do some research and find one that has the mystical attributes to bring you what you are lacking or most need help with at this point in your life.

Gemstones have powerful vibrations, and you are apt to notice the results of this practice quickly. Be consistent though if you really want their vibration integrated into your daily life. I advise against combining different stones together unless or until you have a lot of experience with this technique and a thorough understanding of how the vibrations of stones work together.

Technique for Cultivating Mindfulness (sattva, ether, air, water, and earth)

Here is a solar energy technique for cultivating mindfulness. I'm presenting a few solar techniques in this book because they are difficult to come by from other resources and sun-based techniques work to clarify and strengthen both temperament and overall physical body constitution. Mindfulness refers to the ability to focus on a specific thing in the present moment, which essentially means not perceiving things through the stored impressions of the mind. It will also help teach you the difference in awareness versus experience and how to transition between awareness, feeling, integration, and grounding of energy. To be mindful, you will be able to recognize if you are merely aware of something or if you are experiencing it directly. This will help you to be present in both awareness and experience with all of life's situations.

Stand outside directly in the sunlight on a sunny day. Make sure to do this during times of day when sun exposure is safe and take necessary precautions if you will be in the sun for a long time. Start by focusing on the awareness that you are standing in the sunlight. There is the sun, you, and lots of space in between. Move this perception down into the realm of feeling. Focus on feeling the rays of the sun on your skin through the sense of touch. Take note in your mind how this feels to be touched by the rays of the sun. Have you really felt the sun like this before? Feel the energy being absorbed through your skin and entering into your body. Now, focus on feeling the energy flow through all of the water in your body. Feel the solar energy flow inside of you. Feel what is happening in your body with the influx of solar energy you are present with.

Start by doing this technique for only 3 minutes—1.5 minutes of feeling the energy on your skin and 1.5 minutes of feeling its flow in your body. This will ensure you don't get overwhelmed with the energy. Expand the times on this technique only when you feel comfortable doing so and not for more than a total of 10 minutes for this technique (5 minutes in each phase). Once you are done, walk around peacefully for one minute, if possible with your bare feet on the earth so that you can feel your body connecting directly to the earth, which will assist in grounding.

Technique for Cultivating Intuition & Subtle Awareness (sattva, rajas, earth, air, and ether)

One of the most powerful ways to strengthen intuition and cultivate inner knowing is through meditation. Both silent meditation and meditation techniques work well. Here you will learn a combined visualization and meditation technique to strengthen your connection with yourself.

Sit quietly in a comfortable seated position with your eyes closed. Breathe comfortably and focus on the breath. Take your focus inward to the middle of the chest in the fourth chakra area. Visualize open, blue-black space. Keep the breathing peaceful and focus intently on the visualization. It may not be easy to visualize, but with daily practice, will get easier. Do your best to focus on the visualization and let thoughts and feelings go. You can practice this portion of the technique for 5 to 11 minutes. Once this phase is done, visualize sparkles of color and flashes of light coming out of the darkness in all colors. Make sure these sparkles and flashes of light are tiny in comparison with yourself. Do this visualization for 3 minutes, then sit quietly with a completely blank mind and no visualization for 2 to 3 more minutes.

When people experience intuition or inner knowing, it is described as a spontaneous thing arising out of nothingness. This meditation and visualization will open you up to receiving all spectrums of energy that arise out of nothingness. In fact, if you sit and visualize this field of expansive emptiness long enough, you'll naturally start to notice things appearing within it. This is normal. Practice this technique daily to get the most benefit from it. This is a good technique to practice in the evening or before bed.

Technique for Cultivating Inner Prosperity (sattva, rajas, tamas, and earth)

Inner prosperity relates to sincerely following your life path and having a strong sense of self-worth, which is a very individual process. The roots of prosperity are in love, and in allowing love to flow freely inwardly. This visualization technique will help establish a sense of security deep within the foundation of the chakra system to serve as a platform for allowing all other subtle energies to work.

Sit in a comfortable seated position, either on the floor, on a pillow, or in a chair. What is important is that you feel comfortable and relaxed. Close your eyes and take a few deep breaths in and out. Visualize red and white energy coming together to form a ping-pong to golf-ball sized ball of pink energy sitting in the first (root) chakra. You should see a gentle pink color that is not too bright or vibrant. If it appears very vivid, mix more white light into it so that it is light pink and gentle in nature. Focus on this visualization for 3 to 5 minutes. After the 3 to 5 minutes, let the gentle glow of this pink light sit in the center of the first chakra and visualize wisps of its energy emanating outwardly through the entire first chakra. Once you can clearly see or feel this, visualize wisps of this energy traveling upward through your body, going through the heart center, down your arms, and up into the head. Let the wisps of energy dissipate and disappear quickly; there is no need to hold them there. As they vanish, visualize more of this pink energy gently traveling through your body. Repeat the visualization of the wisps of pink energy for 3 to 5 minutes, then conclude the technique by sitting in silence for at least 2 minutes.

The red energy represents the passions of life and the physical world, whereas the white energy represents the pure essence of God and the highest aspects of each person's inner being. By mixing the two together in a loving way while focusing on the first chakra, you can learn to feel security and love to build solid foundations in life to grow from.

Water Element Cleansing Technique (water)

This technique will combine both visualization and actual water to facilitate a cleansing process within the body. This technique can be used to get rid of negative thoughts and feelings as well as possibly decrease anxiety and stress. Drink a cup of water, then sit in a comfortable seated position. Don't drink more than a cup or it will be difficult to sit peacefully and focus. Take a few deep breaths in and out as you get comfortable. You've just drunk a cup of water; contemplate on the cleansing properties of water to wash away dirt and grime, both literally and energetically. Visualize the subtle essence of the water you've drunk entering into all parts of your subtle body as a cooling, refreshing, and cleansing energy flowing and washing away things that are not in your best interest. There is no need to focus on any specific thing; in fact, don't. Don't draw attention to anything negative in this process. Keep your attention solely on the flow of water and it's washing away of everything that is not within your own inherent nature.

As you as visualizing the water flowing through your body, shift your attention to the second chakra (svadhisthana) area. Begin to visualize yourself sitting on the beach, watching the ocean tides come and go. Watch them start to gently flow over your legs, then feel the tide pulling out everything that is not good for you as the wave returns to the ocean. Witness this process for some time. Try to really feel the gentle waves cleansing the negativity out of you (remember ocean water contains salt, which is naturally purifying and will absorb negativity to carry it away). Do this entire technique between 5 to 8 minutes a day. At the end of the technique sit peacefully for at least 3 more minutes. Once you have completed the technique, go and drink another cup of water before returning to the activities of your day.

Visualization on Infinite Space (ether)

This visualization on infinite space is meant to help you connect with both ether element and the expansiveness of your subtle energy. You can use this technique in different ways. First, work with it consistently to get familiar with the technique. Once you feel comfortable with it and can really feel your subtle energy expanding and contracting, you can use this technique to focus on a particular painful area of your body to help alleviate physical pain. We feel pain when things are constricted; the more space that is added to constriction, the more pain vanishes. This takes practice, but can be accomplished with consistent practice.

Get into a comfortable seated position and relax. Close your eyes and take a few deep breaths in and out. Visualize yourself in your seated position. Visualize yourself going upward, out of your body, up through the clouds, the sky, and off into outer space. Try to still feel the connection with your physical body, but imagine yourself out in the vastness of outer space. See the planets, stars, and galaxies. Keep going out. Keep going until you see nothing but pure blue-black space, void of everything. Sit in this place of void and feel your energy expanding into this void of nothingness for as far as your energy can reach. Do this portion of the technique for 5 minutes. After 5 minutes, visualize your energy coming back together until you are a spot of light amidst the darkness of space. Feel yourself coming back down to your body. Watch yourself pass by the galaxies, stars, and planets—feel yourself coming back to earth and coming all the way into your physical body. Do this second portion of the technique where you are coming back to yourself for 5 minutes. Sit quietly feeling your energy in your physical body for 3 to 5 minutes.

If you have things to do after this technique that require focus (like driving, cooking, or working) you may want to follow up this technique with a grounding exercise. *See "Visualization for Grounding Energy" exercise here in chapter 6.* This will help you regain focus and be fully present with your physical body.

Technique for Cultivating Unity
(sattva, rajas, and tamas)

Within the heart (Hridaya chakra) is where everything is united and working harmoniously together. In order to incorporate a greater sense of unity and interconnection of all things, we will learn a technique that focuses on the heart center.

Sit quietly in a comfortable seated position. Either visualize or feel a lavender energy in the center of the heart. Let this energy grow until it is filling the entire heart. Hold this visualization or feeling with you for as long as you can. Let the energy engulf everything within the heart and all aspects of your being (since everything is contained within the heart). Feel all of your diverse energies coming together as a unified whole in this lavender energy. Let this turn into a meditation technique where you feel this energy working inside of you. End the technique by sitting quietly with no visualization for 3 minutes. This technique can be practiced for 5 to 11 minutes a day.

By practicing this technique consistently, you will gain greater clarity of the inherent unity in all things and feel more deeply unified within yourself. This technique must be practiced consistently every day to have a lasting effect in your life.

Technique for New Growth & Positive Change (sattva, rajas, earth, air, and ether)

We've already learned a technique for cultivating inner prosperity. Let's now learn a technique to stimulate new growth and outer abundance in life. This is excellent to practice together with the *"Technique for Cultivating Inner Prosperity"* we learned earlier, as both will add fuel to each other.

Sit in a comfortable seated position and get relaxed. If you have green things in your home that you enjoy, such as stones, crystals, plants, art, or anything that brings you joy, bring it into your space as you do this technique. Close your eyes and visualize a vibrant emerald green energy swirling in your heart center. Let this energy grow and expand. It can stay vibrant or turn to a dark, rich forest-green color. Let this energy grow roots down into the ground to draw nourishment from the earth. Watch the energy grow and expand. It can take on the shape of a plant or a tree, or remain just as energy, whatever you prefer. See this vibrant green energy as magnetic and drawing external positive energy to you. As you sit and visualize, chant the mantra "shreem hreem hreem shreem." (We learned the shreem bija earlier and its connection to inner prosperity and beauty; the bija hreem will help to attract outer abundance.)

Do this technique for 3 to 8 minutes daily, but not more than 8 minutes. Once you are done, sit quietly for

2 to 3 minutes before you continue the activities of your day. To strengthen this energy even further, eat healthy green foods (leafy greens, spinach, broccoli, green tea, etc.) and spend some time in nature each day.

Conclusion

I hope you've enjoyed diving into this exploration of vibrational healing. In this book, we've walked through all of the foundational concepts necessary to understand what vibrational healing is and how to make it effective in your life. We started by learning the differences between Western medical approaches and vibrational healing and learned how the mind, heart, feelings, and spiritual aspects of life affect health. From there we learned what precisely subtle energy is, where it comes from, and how it moves in the body. We explored ten main chakras necessary to maintain optimum health and life balance. We continued by learning how the subtle energy we carry creates our temperament (gunas) and physical body composition (elements), and how both of these are created in accordance with our individual life paths. You've had the opportunity to take two quizzes to help determine your guna and elemental composition and have been shown how the different parts of the mind, body, and soul work together to make you uniquely you and facilitate balanced living. From there, we explored different types of healing modalities as they relate to both the gunas and the elements. We learned several techniques that work with specific gunas and elements so that you can find a technique that works with your current needs and overall life path.

I hope this book inspires you to go out and try some vibrational healing modalities for yourself! I also hope this book gives you a new way to approach yourself and life as a whole. Healing is very a personal and experiential journey that all comes back to you and your life path. By introducing how these modalities work and giving you a different way to understand yourself, I hope it's easier for you to be courageous and try something new. What did you learn about yourself and the process of healing? How has it changed your perspective on life? This is just the beginning!

Keep exploring, keep learning, and most importantly, keep dreaming. In your dreams you'll find what matters most: yourself. Keep diving deep into yourself and what matters most to you. The limits to life, happiness, and health are as expansive as your own mind! Live well, be well, and to your heart, always be true!

Appendix: For the Healers

Let's explore some concepts of what makes an effective healer. We will look at this from the standpoint of the soul, a person's innate dharma, and the natural gifts we possess. We will discuss how to use our strengths to do the best work possible and how to use the mind, body, soul unified connection to know what to do, how to best do it, and how to work with the process of healing. We will also look at some of the practical matters around health and healing, including ethics and money, and how these can best be dealt with on an individual level.

What Makes an Effective Healer?

I am certain that many of you are contemplating becoming a healer, which is why you've picked up this book. Let's look at some things that will make your journey into understanding vibrational healing meaningful. What does it mean to be an effective healer rather than an ineffective one? How can you tell if you are giving your best or not regarding becoming the best healer you can be?

Healing requires both depth and subtle perception. It requires you to be your best, so that you can give your best to others. It requires that you actively live a unified mind, body, soul connection in everyday life—that this integrated place of balance is your lifestyle, not something you do on the side. First and foremost, you must understand your dharma and overall life path. Be true to your own temperament. If you feel the deep pull to work with people in a healing capacity, then go for it! There are hundreds of ways you can approach healing, so understanding yourself and your inclinations very well is a crucial first step. A yoga therapist works very differently from an acupuncturist, who is different than an energy healer. Each of these people are healers, but their temperaments and overall lifestyles are bound to be vastly different. What makes you happy? What makes your heart come alive and blossom? By understanding these nuances of your character, you can be honest about the lifestyle you want to live and the specific modalities you best resonate with.

Focus on modalities that work well with your own temperament and elemental composition. If you try to focus on modalities you don't enjoy just because you think they are somehow better than the ones that delight you, you've missed the point entirely. It will be very challenging to master a modality that does not work for your own temperament, and it will be even more difficult to be joyful while working with the modality on others. The modalities you will work best with are extensions of your own character. A modality is merely a tool to facilitate a process of healing. You can only truly give that which you are within, so make sure when you are giving of your essence that the modalities you work with resonate with your entire life. This is a matter of utilizing your strengths. Using your strengths and gifts will promote powerful feelings of inner prosperity, which acts as the fuel for everything else good to come from, for yourself and the people you work with.

To be an excellent healer, approach the process of learning like you would a formal education: be serious about your pursuit, take adequate time to learn, and become well-rounded. Having a basic understanding of different areas will allow you to comfortably understand the people you work with and make the best decisions possible for their overall well-being. Effective healers take the time to learn and cultivate their skills in more than one area, although many end up specializing in one particular area to truly master it. Since people are so diverse and since healing requires reaching different levels of the mind, body, soul connection, being able to utilize more than one modality, or at least having the knowledge of what to refer someone to is the quickest way to target a problem. Effective healers also have overall life balance where work is not their sole focus. Having this whole life balance makes understanding more than one modality easier, because life always includes diversity and complexity. It may not seem intuitive at first, but well-cared for individuals who really know themselves and take the time to fulfill areas in all aspects of life, will be the most effective in working with others to help them become healthy and unified. To heal means to make whole. Is your life a focus on wholeness or solely on a single aspect of fulfillment?

There is one practitioner in particular I love to see. He does a combination of massage together with cranial-sacral work and Reiki and knows quite a bit about herbal remedies as well. He has a good work-life balance and a good focus on both family and spirituality. It is clear from the way he approaches his practice that this is his life. He is very effective in his modalities and very effective at making his clientele feel comfortable. Comfort is very important for healing, because it requires an opening up to the unknown.

Once you have a good idea about what modalities you want to do, decide if you want to do healing work as a profession or a hobby. Before you begin practicing healing work on others, understand your relationship to money or any other mode of exchange. Understand why you are a healer and why you want to work with people. Follow your heart and set firm internal guidelines for yourself. This is a heated topic amongst many people, but it need not be. Just be true to yourself. There is nothing wrong with making a living from healing as a profession just as there is nothing wrong with doing healing work on people for free. It comes down to what works for your life and what your goals are.

When I do healing and guidance work, some of it I charge for and some of it I don't. It all depends on the situation at hand, and I always follow my inner guidance. I don't turn people away who can't pay and I also don't work with everyone who comes to me if I don't feel I can really be of benefit to them. The consistency in my approach is that I always listen to my inner guidance and never doubt what it says. Money is never the deciding factor—my heart is. Having a good understanding of yourself and how you relate to your practice and money will free up your energy for the healing work itself and not lock it up in a battle within your own mind.

If it is your choice to be a professional healer, pursue it with your full passion and attention. Ensure that you are competent in your art before you start charging for it. Anytime money comes into the picture, make sure you know your own motivation and have a proper personal code of conduct you adhere to. Let me give you an example. Just because a person goes through a training program does not make them a competent healer. Having a certificate does not make you a healer. It makes you a graduate of a program and a practitioner. It takes time and practice to bring wisdom to your healing gifts, and inner wisdom is an important ingredient of health and healing. Healing comes from depth; it cannot be effective when it remains on the surface and lacks connection with your deepest essence. To ensure you can reach your deepest essence consistently, know exactly how you will deal with all of the superficial things, including money, before you begin. Staying focused and centered will allow you to consistently give your best to your healing work and the people you are working with.

Healer, Heal Thyself!

Nearly all effective healers have had to overcome some health issue or difficulty in their own life. This is part of the natural process of growth that makes people want to heal others. It is important to ensure that you have effectively first healed yourself. No one is perfect, but do the best you can with yourself so that you can joyously give your absolute best to others.

The subtle energy you have will automatically be felt by the people who work with you. If it is loving and accepting, that will be felt. If you have not fully loved yourself and your own struggles, that will also be felt. How well do you interact with people? How do people feel when they are around you? These are important questions to ask. If you don't have the capacity to make someone feel comfortable in your presence, your chances of getting them to open up and allow for deep healing is not likely to happen. When people show discomfort around you, it may be because there are still parts of yourself that need some work. Take the time to honestly assess this and do whatever is required to bring yourself into a state of balance.

Some people think this comes down to grounding before a session. I am not of this mindset. Healers need to walk their walk and talk their talk. Live a healthy lifestyle.

Take care of your mind, body, and soul daily. Have consistency in your own routine. If you yourself have not or cannot do something yourself, how can you ever tell someone else to? As a vibrational healer, people won't come to listen to your words, but to feel the energy you emit. Another person's well-being and maybe even life is in your hands, so take your work seriously and always give your best. Healing requires you to be fully present and put all of your essence into the healing process. The mind cannot be scattered and focused on a hundred different things, like it is in some other forms of work. Until you have calmed the mind and learned to be fully in the here and now, giving your absolute best is not possible. Since vibrational healing deals with very subtle levels of both energy and experience, it takes depth and focus to do it well. If your own life is not in order, you will face challenges in your healing work.

Healing Comes from Within

This is probably the most important concept for all healers to understand. Health and healing is always a process that comes from within. Even if you are the greatest healer in the world, you won't have the capacity to heal everyone that comes to you. Every individual has to in their own heart and mind accept the healing vibrations coming to them. We all have free will to either be healthy or to hold onto disease. Many people don't consciously want to hold onto disease, but somewhere inside the subconscious is a reason to experience the pain or suffering.

The willingness and ability to let go must be greater than the ability to hold onto disease.

Healing is about giving, not ego and not forcing. Healers and the variety of modalities available are merely conduits for energy to travel through. That's right; you are just a conduit. It's a beautiful process of giving energy to another person so they have help in their journey. Why people choose on some level to not heal is a part of their personal life journey on a soul level, and these choices have to be accepted and respected. As the healer, you are only half of this equation. A person who is not healed is not to blame for this, and neither is the healer. Some things are beyond understanding. Just do your best, give your best always, and show compassion always.

If you are only a conduit as a healer, what can you do to be the most effective healer possible? Since healing is a process of giving and receiving, contemplate how you can really open up inwardly in such a way that invites people to step into their own power and healing potential. Your job is not only to be a master at your chosen modality, but to carry yourself in such a way that inspires others to also become their best. It's this inner energy, the inner prosperity that you carry, that will either draw people to you or push people away. It's your energy that will help them to open up and receive the vibration you are sharing with them.

This process is not fully a conscious choice. The gunas we have interact with the gunas in other people in such a way that your energy will always either inspire or constrict other people. It's your responsibility as an effective healer to ensure your energy is supportive of the healing process of everyone who comes to you. This goes far beyond conscious awareness and intention down into the subconscious levels of the energy you carry. Both your conscious and subconscious energies will interact with the people you work with.

There are different ways to be inspirational and it comes down to your own temperament and character development. This is something for you to deeply reflect on so that you can become the best "you" possible! Enjoy the process of growth and learning. There are few rewards in life greater than being able to help someone else in need. As a healer, you are certain to impact people far beyond what you can comprehend and you will definitely change yourself too. May health, happiness, and inner prosperity always be a part of your journey, and may you bless and heal many, many people with your presence, character and abilities!

Recommended Reading

Andrews, Ted. *The Healer's Manual: a Beginner's Guide to Energy Therapies.* St. Paul, MN: Llewellyn Publications, 1993.

Andrews, Ted. *Nature-Speak: Signs, Omens and Messages in Nature.* Jackson, TN: Dragonhawk Pub., 2004.

Bharadwaj, Monisha. *The Indian Spice Kitchen: Essential Ingredients and Over 200 Authentic Recipes.* New York: Dutton, 1996.

Frawley, David. *Ayurveda and the Mind: the Healing of Consciousness.* Twin Lakes, WI: Lotus Press, 1996.

Frawley, David. *Mantra Yoga and Primal Sound: Secrets of Seed (Bija) Mantras.* Twin Lakes, WI: Lotus Press, 2010.

Hall, Judy. *The Crystal Bible.* Cincinnati, OH: Walking Stick Press, 2003.

The Mother. *Flowers and Their Messages.* Silver Lake, WI: Lotus Light Publications, 1992.

Shumsky, Susan. *Exploring Chakras.* Franklin Lakes, NJ: New Page Books, 2003.

Other Resources

Pathways Health Crisis Resource Center. http://www.pathwaysminneapolis.org/

Gita for the Masses. http://www.gitaforthemasses.org

American Institute of Vedic Studies. http://www.vedanet.com

To Write the Author

If you wish to contact the author or would like more information about this book, please write to the author in care of Llewellyn Worldwide, and we will forward your request. Both the author and publisher appreciate hearing from you and learning of your enjoyment of this book and how it has helped you. Llewellyn Worldwide cannot guarantee that every letter written to the author can be answered, but all will be forwarded. Please write to:

Jaya Jaya Myra
⁒ Llewellyn Worldwide
2143 Wooddale Drive
Woodbury, MN 55125-2989

Please enclose a self-addressed stamped envelope for reply, or $1.00 to cover costs. If outside the USA, enclose an international postal reply coupon.